JASVIR SINGH

Raising Kids Without Smartphones

How to Build Confident, Resilient Children in a Digital World

NDJ PRESS

Contents

Acknowledgments

First, to my children — thank you. You are the reason these questions matter. Your curiosity, your frustration, your growth, and your resilience have shaped my thinking far more than any study ever could. You have taught me that development cannot be rushed and that maturity unfolds quietly. This book exists because I am watching you grow.

To my family, for your patience and steadiness. Conversations at the dinner table, thoughtful disagreements about timing, quiet recalibrations, and shared reflection helped shape the ideas within these pages. Growth is rarely dramatic; it is built through repetition. You have lived that repetition with grace.

To the parents who shared their doubts and experiences — thank you for your honesty. Many of you spoke openly about uncertainty, pressure, and moments you wished you had handled differently. Your candor is a reminder that parenting in this era is less about perfection and more about thoughtful leadership.

To educators and mentors who guide children through complexity — your influence reaches further than test scores. While schools teach knowledge, you shape character. That work is immeasurable.

And finally, to every parent reading this book: your willingness to pause and reflect already speaks volumes. The fact that you are considering timing, maturity, and emotional development is evidence of care. Thoughtful parenting may not receive applause, but it leaves a lasting imprint.

This book was written with deep respect for your courage — the courage to remain steady in a fast-moving world.

The Digital Readiness Ladder

Before a child holds a smartphone,
they must learn to hold themselves.
Access is easy.
Strength is built.
A device does not create maturity.
It magnifies what is already there.
Weak self-control becomes constant distraction.
Fragile identity becomes endless comparison.
Undeveloped judgment becomes borrowed thinking.
Sequence matters.
You cannot build confidence without discernment.
You cannot develop discernment without responsibility.
You cannot sustain responsibility without discipline.
You cannot practice discipline without emotional regulation.
You cannot regulate emotion without self-control.

RAISING KIDS WITHOUT SMARTPHONES

— THE LONG VIEW FRAMEWORK —

The foundation is **Self-Control** —

the ability to pause, to wait, to withstand discomfort.

Then **Emotional Regulation** —

mastery over feelings instead of surrender to them.

Then **Discipline** —

choosing what is needed over what is easy.

Then **Responsibility** —

owning actions and their consequences.

Then **Discernment** —

seeing clearly in a world designed to distract.

And finally, **Confidence** —

not built on applause,

but anchored in identity.

This ladder cannot be skipped.

It cannot be rushed.

It cannot be outsourced to a device.

Technology should amplify strength —

not compensate for its absence.

Build the foundation first.

Then hand over the screen.

A Digital Readiness Blessing

Before the screen fits in your hand,

may steadiness live in your heart.
  Before the world can see your words,
  may you know who you are without applause.
  Before notifications call your name,
  may you learn the sound of your own voice.
  Before you measure worth in numbers,
  may you measure it in character.
  Before you chase the crowd,
  may you practice standing still.
  Before comparison flickers across your mind,
  may you feel secure in your becoming.
  Before the scroll becomes endless,
  may your attention be intentional.
  Before access becomes automatic,
  may wisdom come first.

And when the day finally comes
  that the device rests in your palm,

may it amplify your strength —
  not define it.

— Jasvir Singh

Introduction

The Night "Everyone Else" Arrived

It didn't begin with rebellion.

No slammed doors.

No dramatic speeches.

No ultimatums.

It began with a sentence so ordinary it almost slipped past me.

"Everyone else has one."

My child didn't even look up. Just traced a line on the kitchen counter with one finger. Casual. Almost bored.

But it wasn't casual.

Because I knew what that sentence really meant.

It wasn't about a phone.

It was about belonging.

And suddenly I wasn't deciding about a device.

I was deciding about my child's place in the social world.

In that moment, your mind moves fast.

You imagine lunch tables.

Birthday parties.

Inside jokes that circulate at 10:47 p.m.

Group chats forming without your child.

Plans shifting in seconds.

You imagine your child arriving late — not physically, but socially.

And then the question hits:

Am I protecting my child... or isolating them?

Parents rarely admit how heavy this moment feels.

You are not weighing screen time.

You are weighing social survival.

The culture does not slow down to let you think.

In many communities, smartphones appear by fifth or sixth grade. Sometimes earlier.

Group chats begin before adolescence.

Parents quietly compare timelines.

Children quietly compare status.

And underneath it all sits a quiet fear:

If I wait, will my child fall behind?

Here is what almost no one says clearly:

The real issue is not the phone.

The real issue is whether your child has internal footing before stepping into a world that never goes quiet.

Because the world they are entering is not neutral.

It is fast.

It is comparative.

It is visible.

It is permanent.

Notifications don't just inform — they stimulate.

Group chats don't just coordinate — they accelerate.

Social media doesn't just connect — it evaluates.

We are giving children performance tools before identity tools.

We are accelerating access faster than we are building regulation.

And we are calling it normal.

For adults, this environment is exhausting.

For children whose brains are still developing impulse control, emotional regulation, and identity stability, it can be destabilizing when introduced too early.

That is not alarmism.

That is developmental timing.

Neuroscience consistently shows that executive function — the brain's capacity to pause, evaluate, and regulate — continues strengthening into the mid-teen years. Digital platforms, by contrast, are engineered for immediacy.

That mismatch matters.

But this book is not about panic.

It is about preparation.

When I began paying close attention to families navigating this decision, I noticed something unexpected.

The children who delayed were not socially doomed.

They were not friendless.

They were not excluded from life.

What they experienced instead was friction.

They occasionally had to ask, "What time?"

They occasionally missed a joke.

They occasionally felt half a step behind.

But something else developed quietly.

They learned to speak up.

To clarify.

To tolerate being slightly different.

To sit with mild discomfort instead of escaping it instantly.

Those skills are not flashy.

They do not trend.

They do not earn likes.

But they build steadiness.

And steadiness becomes protection.

This book is not anti-technology.

It is anti-premature immersion.

Your child will live in a digital world.

That is not optional.

The question is sequencing.

Do we introduce unlimited social access before emotional regulation is stable?

Or do we build strength first — then expand access?

Build strength before screens.

That is the philosophy at the center of this book.

There is a difference between exposure and readiness.

A difference between connection and dependence.

A difference between fitting in and belonging.

Belonging rooted in internal confidence is steady.

Belonging rooted in constant feedback is fragile.

Fragile belonging requires constant checking.

Steady belonging can tolerate silence.

Delaying a smartphone is not about winning an argument.

It is about building internal muscles first.

The muscle of boredom — generating stimulation from within.

The muscle of self-advocacy — asking directly instead of passively waiting.

The muscle of emotional regulation — tolerating being left out occasionally without unraveling.

The muscle of real-world conversation — navigating tone, eye contact, and repair.

These muscles form slowly.

And once built, they change everything.

This book will not give you a rigid rule.

It will not promise that delaying guarantees confidence.

It will not pretend that every child develops at the same pace.

Instead, it will give you clarity.

You will understand what actually changes when smartphones arrive early.

You will learn what readiness truly means.

You will learn how to delay without triggering power struggles.

You will learn how to say yes without surrendering structure.

And if you have already said yes, you will learn how to recalibrate without guilt.

The culture will continue accelerating.

Platforms will change.

Apps will evolve.

Trends will rotate faster than we can name them.

Your child's developmental needs will not change.

They will still need sleep.

They will still need conversation.

They will still need boundaries.

They will still need practice tolerating discomfort.

They will still need to know they can belong without constantly performing.

The device is not the foundation.

Your child's internal stability is.

There will come a day when your child receives a smartphone.

When that day arrives, the goal is not relief.

It is readiness.

Not urgency.

But maturity.

This is not about keeping them behind.

It is about helping them stand steady when they step forward.

Build strength first.

Then expand access.

Let's begin there.

1

The Myth of "Everyone Else"

The sentence rarely arrives with drama.

It slips into conversation as if it has been rehearsed quietly in your child's mind.

"Everyone else has one."

They may not look at you when they say it.

They might say it while scrolling on a shared tablet.

Or from the back seat of the car.

Or between bites of dinner, as if the words are casual.

They are not casual.

Because beneath that sentence is a deeper question your child may not yet have language for:

Am I falling behind?

Not academically.

Not athletically.

Socially.

"Everyone" Is Emotional, Not Statistical

When children say "everyone," they are not conducting a census.

They are measuring proximity.

They mean the children who matter most in their daily world — the ones at their lunch table, the teammates in their circles, the classmates who seem socially central.

A handful of visible, confident children can create the illusion of universality.

If the socially active kids have smartphones, it can feel like the entire world does.

Silence reinforces that illusion.

The children who are waiting rarely announce it. There is no roll call for "Who doesn't have one yet?"

So the mind fills in the gap.

Everyone must have one.

But even if many do, that still does not answer the real question underneath the sentence:

Will I still belong without it?

Belonging Feels Like Safety

Belonging is not trivial in childhood.

It feels like safety.

Developmental psychology consistently shows that peer acceptance during late childhood and early adolescence strongly influences self-esteem and emotional regulation. The social brain is highly active during this stage. Feedback from peers carries weight.

To be inside the group feels secure.

To feel slightly outside — even temporarily — can feel destabilizing.

So when your child asks for a smartphone, they are often asking for protection against exclusion.

And when you hesitate, you are not hesitating about technology.

You are hesitating about timing.

The tension between protection and preparation sits at the center of this decision.

Access Is Not Stability

A smartphone offers access — access to conversation, coordination, inside jokes, shared media, constant updates.

But access is not the same as stability.

A child can be deeply embedded in a group chat and still feel uncertain about where they stand.

They can receive constant notifications and still worry that they are one misstep away from exclusion.

Speed feels powerful.

But speed is not depth.

Depth is built through shared experience, face-to-face interaction, mutual trust, and time.

Technology can amplify connection.

It does not manufacture security.

Why Data Doesn't Calm the Fear

Many parents respond to "everyone else" with data.

They cite statistics.

They mention age averages.

They explain that not every child has one.

But data does not compete with proximity.

Your child is not worried about national percentages.

They are worried about the five children who shape their daily reality.

Responding with statistics can make them feel dismissed.

Responding with anger can make them feel ashamed.

Responding with panic confirms the urgency.

The most stabilizing first response is acknowledgment:

"It makes sense that you'd feel that way."

That sentence lowers defenses.

It does not promise a device.

It communicates understanding.

Understanding buys you time.
Time builds maturity.

Look Beneath the Sentence

Before making any decision, ask a different question:
What feels hardest about waiting?
Is it missing last-minute plan changes?
Not knowing the time of practice?
Feeling embarrassed to say, "I don't have a phone yet"?
Fear that friendships will drift?
Each fear has a different solution.
Logistics can be solved with structure.
Embarrassment can be softened with language.
Friendship concerns can be addressed with intentional connection.
When you explore what is underneath the sentence, the urgency often decreases.

Parent Anxiety Is Real Too

Sometimes the anxiety belongs as much to the parent as to the child.
You may remember your own middle school years.
The invisible hierarchies.
The sharp edges of exclusion.
You imagine your child reliving those moments — amplified by screens.
Your nervous system reacts.
That instinct is loving.
But urgency can distort clarity.
Not every inconvenience is harm.
There is a difference between isolation and friction.
Isolation is sustained exclusion — no invitations, no inclusion, no belonging.
Friction is inconvenience — arriving slightly late to a plan, hearing about a

joke afterward, asking for clarification.

Friction is uncomfortable.

It is not catastrophic.

In fact, mild friction builds social skill.

A child who learns to say, "Can you tell me the time again?" is practicing self-advocacy.

A child who learns to tolerate being slightly out of sync is building resilience.

Those micro-skills accumulate.

The Long Game

Zoom out further.

What kind of internal life do you want your child to have at fifteen?

Do you want them to feel steady if a message goes unanswered for hours?

Do you want them to tolerate occasional exclusion without spiraling?

Do you want them capable of initiating plans directly rather than waiting passively for updates?

The decision at ten does not determine everything.

But it shapes patterns.

And patterns, repeated over years, shape identity.

If a child learns early that inclusion depends on constant digital presence, that association can become internalized.

If a child learns that belonging can exist even when they are not constantly connected, that becomes internalized too.

Developmental Timing

This is not about moral superiority.

It is about developmental sequencing.

Research in child and adolescent development consistently shows that executive function — impulse control, emotional regulation, long-term thinking — continues strengthening throughout early adolescence.

Meanwhile, smartphones introduce:

Continuous feedback.

Continuous comparison.

Continuous availability.

Those demands require regulation.

When regulation precedes exposure, the transition tends to be smoother.

When exposure precedes regulation, children practice self-control under social pressure.

Some adapt well.

Some quietly struggle.

The device itself is not the villain.

The timing is the variable.

Not Never. Not Yet.

Your child may say it is unfair.

They may compare you to other parents.

They may insist that you do not understand.

That does not mean your approach is wrong.

It means you are holding a boundary in a culture that moves quickly.

Boundaries, when held calmly, communicate confidence.

Confidence transfers.

If you speak about delay with anxiety, your child absorbs anxiety.

If you speak about delay with steadiness, your child borrows that steadiness.

"We're not against phones. We're preparing for them."

That framing shifts the conversation from prohibition to development.

Not never.

Not yet.

Reframing "Everyone"

Delayed does not mean deprived.

It can mean developed.

Your child may repeat the sentence many times.

Each time is not an argument to win.
It is an opportunity to reinforce foundation.
Belonging built on internal confidence is durable.
Belonging built solely on access is fragile.
The myth of "everyone" feels overwhelming up close.
It shrinks when you widen the lens.
You are not behind.
You are choosing timing deliberately.
And deliberate timing is not weakness.

It is leadership.

2

What Actually Happens When Smartphones Arrive Early

When parents imagine giving their child a smartphone, they usually picture relief.

Relief from logistical confusion.

Relief from last-minute plan changes.

Relief from the fear of exclusion.

Relief from constant requests.

They imagine smoother coordination.

They imagine gratitude.

They imagine peace.

And often, at first, that's exactly what happens.

The tension drops.

The arguments quiet.

Your child feels current — inside the flow of their social world instead of slightly outside it.

It feels like a solution.

But what often goes unnoticed is what begins quietly alongside that relief.

Not catastrophe.

Not immediate crisis.

But subtle shifts.

And subtle shifts, repeated daily, shape development.

The First Week: The Honeymoon

The early days are usually smooth.

Your child joins the group chat.

They send their first meme.

They check messages after school.

They no longer need to ask, "What time?" as often.

They feel synced.

You feel less worried.

But beneath the surface, three new forces enter their daily life immediately:

Continuous access.

Continuous comparison.

Continuous availability.

These three forces reshape childhood more than most families anticipate.

Continuous Access

Before a smartphone, access has natural boundaries.

School ends.

Practice ends.

You come home.

The door closes.

There is separation between environments.

With a smartphone, that separation disappears.

School follows your child home.

So does group drama.

So do inside jokes.

So does subtle exclusion.

So do shifting alliances.

Even if nothing dramatic is happening, the possibility of something happening keeps attention partially engaged.

The brain stays slightly alert.

There may be no active conversation.

But there could be.

Psychologists sometimes describe this as ambient vigilance — a low-level state of alertness that never fully powers down.

For a developing nervous system, that matters.

Continuous Comparison

Childhood has always included comparison.

Who runs faster.

Who gets invited first.

Who reads more fluently.

Smartphones intensify comparison visually and constantly.

Now there are:

Photos curated for reaction.

Messages that receive more replies.

Inside jokes that exclude.

Response times that feel meaningful.

Silences that feel deliberate.

Social comparison theory has long shown that humans evaluate themselves relative to others — especially when identity is forming.

Pre-adolescence is a fragile identity period.

When comparison becomes constant, evaluation becomes constant.

Instead of asking, "What do I think?"

Children begin asking, "How did that land?"

Instead of asking, "Do I like this?"

They ask, "Will this get a reaction?"

This shift is subtle.

But it moves identity from internally anchored to externally calibrated.

That does not happen in a week.

It happens slowly, through repetition.

Continuous Availability

Before smartphones, communication required proximity or planning.
Now it requires only a notification.
Friends expect quick responses.
Group chats move rapidly.
Plans shift mid-evening.
When a child does not respond quickly, they may feel behind.
When they respond too quickly, they may feel exposed.
Availability becomes performance.
And performance is tiring.
Adults feel this exhaustion.
Imagine an eleven-year-old navigating it daily.
The pressure to be reachable can quietly erode the ability to disconnect.

The Sleep Shift

One of the earliest measurable changes after smartphone introduction is sleep.
Even in families with "no phones in bedrooms" rules, patterns shift.
Why?
Because anticipation alters behavior.
Children check devices before bed.
They think about what might be happening.
They replay conversations.
They wait for responses.
The house is quiet.
At 11:30 p.m., a faint vibration hums through the hallway.
Not loud. Just enough.
You pause outside the bedroom door.
Another buzz.
You wonder — is it homework? A joke? A shift in a group plan?
You stand there longer than you expected.

Sleep becomes lighter.

Less restorative.

Research consistently shows that reduced sleep affects emotional regulation, impulse control, and mood stability — especially in adolescents.

A tired child is more reactive.

More sensitive to minor social slights.

More likely to misinterpret tone.

Sometimes what parents describe as "attitude" is cumulative fatigue.

And fatigue compounds.

The Acceleration Effect

Smartphones accelerate social dynamics.

Before digital group chats, conflicts unfolded face-to-face.

Tone softened misunderstandings.

Shared physical space provided context.

Now misunderstandings scale quickly.

Screenshots circulate.

Comments spread.

Private remarks become public.

Children are asked to process complex social layers earlier than their emotional regulation systems may comfortably manage.

Acceleration can look like maturity.

But acceleration without regulation often feels overwhelming.

Externally savvy.

Internally strained.

The Quiet Loss of Boredom

Boredom is one of childhood's most underrated developmental tools.

Before smartphones, boredom prompted imagination.

Children invented games.

Built things.

Read.

Talked.

Or simply sat.

Unstructured time builds self-generated stimulation.

With a smartphone, boredom has an immediate solution:

Scroll.

Check.

Refresh.

Instead of asking, "What can I create?"

The child asks, "What's new?"

The ability to tolerate boredom strongly correlates with creativity, focus, and emotional resilience later in life.

When novelty becomes the default coping mechanism, internal resourcefulness gets less practice.

Not because the child lacks ability.

Because the environment reduces opportunity.

Emotional Regulation Under Pressure

Smartphones introduce rapid emotional fluctuations.

A laugh.

A reaction.

A message.

A silence.

A perceived slight.

A change of plan.

Each is minor.

But repeated dozens of times per day, the emotional system cycles more frequently.

Adults struggle with this.

Preteens are still learning to label and regulate emotion.

When emotional fluctuation increases without corresponding maturity, mood volatility often follows.

Parents may observe:

Irritability.

Withdrawal.

Overreaction to small events.

Heightened sensitivity.

The phone did not create those traits.

It amplified them.

Technology magnifies what is already forming.

The Illusion of Social Solution

Many parents hope a smartphone will solve social insecurity.

If my child has access, they won't feel left out.

If they're in the group chat, they'll feel secure.

If they can respond quickly, they'll belong.

But belonging is not built on speed.

It is built on mutual trust and shared experience.

A child who struggles with self-esteem may struggle digitally too — sometimes more.

A child who seeks reassurance may seek it through notifications.

Technology does not cure insecurity.

It often gives it new material.

The Maturity Gap

The largest issue with early smartphone access is not exposure.

It is mismatch.

Mismatch between neurological development and digital demand.

Executive function — the brain's regulation system — strengthens gradually through adolescence.

Digital platforms are engineered for immediate engagement.

Notifications trigger dopamine release.

Algorithms reward frequent checking.

For adults, this requires discipline.
For children, it requires capacity that may still be forming.
When mismatch persists, strain follows.
Sometimes visible.
Sometimes quiet.

Two Different Foundations

Imagine two twelve-year-olds.
Child A receives a smartphone at nine.
Child B receives one at thirteen.
By thirteen, Child A has four years of digital comparison history.
Four years of group chat hierarchies.
Four years of notification conditioning.
Four years of accelerated exposure.
Child B has four years of slower social development.
Four years of in-person coordination.
Four years of boredom tolerance.
Four years of building regulation before immersion.
Neither child is guaranteed stability.
But their foundations differ.
Foundations shape trajectory.

This Is Not Fear

This chapter is not a warning that early smartphones ruin childhood.
Many children receive them at ten or eleven and function reasonably well.
But reasonable is not the same as optimal.
The real question is not:
Will my child survive?
It is:
What developmental trade am I making?
Every family makes trade-offs.

Convenience now.

Capacity later.

Relief now.

Regulation later.

Clarity allows intentional choice.

The Long View

If a smartphone expands your child's world — increasing responsibility, independence, and opportunity — it may be well-timed.

If it shrinks their world — increasing comparison, distraction, and anxiety — it may be premature.

The device is not inherently good or bad.

It is powerful.

Power requires readiness.

And readiness is developmental.

When timing aligns with capacity, integration is smoother.

When timing outruns capacity, strain accumulates.

You are not deciding whether your child will enter the digital world.

They will.

You are deciding when.

And when matters.

3

The Emotional Cost of Constant Connection

A smartphone is not just a communication tool.

It is an emotional environment.

For adults, that environment can feel overwhelming.

For children — whose emotional systems are still developing — it can quietly reshape how they experience belonging, rejection, confidence, and self-worth.

This chapter is not about alarm.

It is about awareness.

Because the emotional cost of constant connection is rarely dramatic at first.

It is cumulative.

The Nervous System Was Not Designed for This Pace

For most of human history, social interaction had boundaries.

You saw people face-to-face.

You interpreted tone through voice and expression.

You experienced conflict — then separation.

You had natural pauses.

Digital environments remove those pauses.

There is no bell ending the day.

No bus ride decompressing the afternoon.

No physical distance softening tension.

Instead:

Messages arrive at night.

Plans shift mid-evening.

Group chats continue while homework is unfinished.

Photos circulate instantly.

Conversations never fully close.

The nervous system stays slightly activated.

Not panicked.

Just elevated.

That low-level elevation, sustained over time, becomes baseline.

And baseline matters.

Micro-Stress Accumulates

Most emotional strain related to smartphones does not look like crisis.

It looks like:

Waiting for someone to respond.

Re-reading a message to interpret tone.

Checking who reacted.

Noticing you were not tagged in a photo.

Seeing plans unfold without you.

Each moment is small.

But children experience them intensely because identity is still forming.

During pre-adolescence, the brain becomes highly sensitive to peer evaluation. Research shows increased activation in regions associated with social processing during this stage.

In simple terms: children feel social feedback more deeply than adults.

So when a message goes unanswered, it does not feel neutral.

It feels meaningful.

And meaning triggers emotion.

The "On Read" Effect

Before smartphones, silence was ambiguous.

If someone did not respond, you could assume they were busy.

Now, silence is visible.

"Seen."

"Read."

The platform confirms that your message was received.

When no reply follows, the brain searches for explanation.

Children may ask themselves:

Did I say something wrong?

Are they annoyed?

Are they talking about me privately?

Was that embarrassing?

Often, the explanation is simple.

Homework. Dinner. A forgotten phone.

But the adolescent brain is wired to interpret social silence as potential threat.

The device amplifies that instinct.

Without emotional maturity to buffer interpretation, children can spiral quickly.

She watches the screen.

Her message sits beneath a small gray word: Seen.

The chat continues above it — jokes, replies, a new plan forming.

No one responds to her line.

She reads it again.

It didn't sound strange when she typed it.

Now it feels louder than it did five minutes ago.

She sets the phone down.

Picks it up again.

The Comparison Spiral

Social comparison did not begin with smartphones.

But smartphones made comparison constant.

Children see:

Group photos.

Filtered images.

Vacation highlights.

Birthday celebrations.

Inside jokes captured mid-laughter.

They do not see:

The arguments before the photo.

The boredom after the party.

The insecurities beneath the smile.

When raw reality is compared to curated highlights, dissatisfaction grows.

Not because life is worse.

Because the comparison is incomplete.

Research consistently links high levels of comparison-driven social media engagement with lower self-esteem and increased anxiety in adolescents.

This does not mean all use is harmful.

It means vulnerability exists.

And timing influences how well a child can manage that vulnerability.

Fear of Missing Out Is Attachment Anxiety

FOMO is often dismissed as vanity.

It is not.

It is attachment anxiety.

It sounds like:

What if something important happens without me?

What if they decide something and I don't know?

What if I fall behind socially?

Belonging equals safety for a child.

The smartphone offers the illusion of monitoring belonging constantly.

But monitoring is not the same as security.

It often increases vigilance.

And vigilance is exhausting.

Children may check repeatedly not because they enjoy it, but because uncertainty feels threatening.

Performance Replaces Presence

In digital spaces, subtle performance pressure emerges.

Will this get reactions?

Is this funny enough?

Will this be screenshot?

Is this embarrassing?

Instead of asking, "Is this honest?" children may ask, "Will this land?"

Identity formation becomes partially external.

When children curate themselves before they fully know themselves, development shifts.

Self-expression becomes strategic.

Spontaneity decreases.

Guardedness increases.

Some children withdraw.

Some over-perform.

Neither response feels steady.

Sleep Disruption and Emotional Volatility

Sleep is one of the most underestimated factors in emotional stability.

Even when devices are not used late at night, anticipation affects rest.

Children may:

Think about what they might miss.

Rehearse conversations.

Wait for responses.

Check "one more time."

Research consistently shows that adolescents who sleep fewer hours exhibit increased irritability, reduced impulse control, and heightened anxiety.

Parents may observe:

Mood swings.

Sensitivity to minor criticism.

Overreaction to small conflicts.

Sometimes the underlying issue is not personality.

It is exhaustion.

And exhaustion lowers emotional resilience.

Conflict Escalates Faster Online

In person, tone softens conflict.

A smile clarifies sarcasm.

Eye contact reduces tension.

Shared history provides context.

Online, tone flattens.

Sarcasm reads as cruelty.

Teasing feels sharper.

Jokes escalate quickly.

Screenshots circulate.

Side conversations form.

Group chats amplify disagreement.

Children may wake up to:

A rumor spreading.

A message taken out of context.

A joke misinterpreted.

They must process that emotional weight before breakfast.

That acceleration requires maturity.

Not all children have built that capacity yet.

The Illusion of Constant Togetherness

Group chats create the impression that everyone is always connected.
But most children are not reading every message.
They mute threads.
They skim.
They miss things.
Still, the illusion persists.
If I am not checking, I am falling behind.
Compulsive checking becomes coping.
Coping becomes habit.
Habit becomes dependency.
Not because children are weak.
Because the design rewards it.

Emotional Dependence on Feedback

One of the more subtle risks of early smartphone immersion is the shift from internal regulation to external validation.
A child feels uncertain.
They post.
They wait for reaction.
The reaction soothes.
Over time, the nervous system pairs validation with relief.
Without validation, discomfort lingers longer.
That pairing strengthens neural pathways.
That is how habits form.
The goal is not to eliminate digital feedback.
It is to ensure internal regulation precedes reliance on it.

Some Children Seem Fine

It is important to say this clearly.

Some children adapt to early smartphone access without obvious difficulty.

They have strong offline friendships.

They have stable self-esteem.

They regulate emotion well.

They have structured households with clear boundaries.

But even resilient children can internalize subtle comparison pressure over time.

The absence of visible crisis does not guarantee emotional ease.

The question is not whether your child can handle it for a month.

It is whether constant exposure shapes their internal narrative over years.

Strength Before Immersion

Delaying a smartphone is not about fear of technology.

It is about strengthening emotional muscles first.

Before full digital immersion, children benefit from practicing:

Handling exclusion face-to-face.

Repairing conflict in person.

Tolerating boredom without escape.

Waiting without instant feedback.

Expressing emotion without broadcasting it.

These skills transfer directly to digital life.

Without them, digital intensity feels heavier.

With them, digital interaction feels manageable.

The Core Question

Before introducing constant connection, ask yourself:

If social life becomes louder, will my child become steadier — or shakier?

There is no perfect moment.

But there is preparation.

Preparation builds internal security.

Security reduces reactivity.

Reduced reactivity changes digital experience entirely.

The smartphone is not inherently harmful.

But constant connection carries emotional cost.

The earlier it begins, the longer that cost accumulates.

Timing shapes trajectory.

And trajectory shapes identity.

4

Group Chats, Social Hierarchies, and the New Playground

If smartphones are the device, group chats are the environment.

For many children, group chats are not simply communication tools.

They are the new playground.

The new cafeteria table.

The new bus ride home.

The new whisper circle.

The new rumor mill.

The new after-school hangout.

The difference is this:

This playground never closes.

The Invisible Architecture of Group Chats

From the outside, a group chat appears harmless.

A string of names.

A stream of messages.

Memes. Homework reminders. Weekend plans.

But inside that stream, hierarchies form quickly.

There is often:

The initiator — who starts conversations.

The entertainer — whose jokes get reactions.

The dominant voice — who sets the tone.

The observer — who reads but rarely speaks.

The ignored — whose comments pass without response.

Children are exquisitely sensitive to these patterns.

Status inside the chat can begin to feel like status in real life.

And because these dynamics unfold privately, adults rarely see them.

Speed Equals Influence

In group chats, speed matters.

Who responds first?

Who gets the most reactions?

Whose message resets the conversation?

Whose comment gets skipped?

The pace of response subtly shapes influence.

Children who think before speaking may feel behind.

Children who are witty and impulsive may rise quickly.

The thoughtful child may feel invisible.

The anxious child may overthink.

The socially bold child may gain dominance.

None of this is inherently good or bad.

But it accelerates hierarchy formation.

And acceleration changes social learning.

The "Left on Read" Experience

One of the most destabilizing experiences for preteens is not being insulted.

It is being ignored.

A child sends a message.

It sits.

Others continue talking.

No one responds.

In person, silence has context.

Someone may be distracted.

Someone may not hear.

In a group chat, silence feels deliberate.

Children may begin asking:

Did I say something wrong?

Are they annoyed?

Am I boring?

Did they screenshot that?

Often, the explanation is simple.

But the adolescent brain is wired to interpret social ambiguity as potential threat.

Repeated exposure to visible silence can quietly erode confidence.

He types the joke quickly.

It felt funny when he thought of it.

He hits send.

The message lands in the thread.

No reactions.

No replies.

Conversation shifts.

He presses and holds the bubble.

Deletes it.

No one says anything.

But he does not forget.

The Screenshot Culture

In previous generations, most childhood conversations disappeared after they ended.

Now they can be captured.

Saved.

Forwarded.

Shared out of context.
Children know this.
Even if they cannot articulate it, they feel it.
That awareness changes behavior.
Some become cautious and guarded.
Some become performative.
Some become reckless, assuming permanence does not apply to them.
The presence of a potential invisible audience shifts communication.
Spontaneity decreases.
Self-monitoring increases.
For a developing identity, that matters.

Side Chats and Visible Exclusion

Group chats rarely remain intact.
Side chats form.
Smaller groups branch off.
Inside jokes migrate.
A child may see:
"Added Ava."
"Added Marcus."
"Added Jordan."
And notice their own name missing.
In earlier eras, exclusion could be suspected.
Now it can be confirmed.
Visible exclusion carries more emotional weight than imagined exclusion.
Ambiguity sometimes protects.
Certainty can wound.

Plans Form in Real Time

Spontaneity is one of the most common stress points.

"Let's go to the park."

"Now?"

"Yeah."

"Meet at four."

A plan forms in seconds.

If your child is not in the thread, they may find out later.

If they are in the thread but not acknowledged, they may watch the plan unfold without invitation.

Both experiences can sting.

Not because the park matters.

Because belonging does.

Repeated small exclusions accumulate into narrative:

I'm not central.

I'm optional.

I'm peripheral.

Narratives shape identity.

Humor and Escalation

Humor travels fast in group chats.

Sarcasm.

Inside jokes.

Teasing.

But tone does not travel well.

Without facial expression and voice modulation, humor sharpens.

What lands gently in person can land harshly online.

Children must interpret tone without cues.

They must decide:

Is this playful?

Should I respond?

Should I defend myself?

Will defending myself make it worse?

These are advanced social decisions.

Many adults struggle with them.

Children are asked to navigate them daily.

The Social Currency of Being "In"

Being inside a group chat carries symbolic weight.

It signals inclusion.

It signals access.

It signals relevance.

Children may tolerate discomfort simply to remain inside the thread.

They may laugh at jokes they do not find funny.

They may stay silent when something feels wrong.

They may join teasing to avoid becoming the target.

Belonging pressure can override personal values.

The digital environment amplifies conformity.

The Child Without Access

When a child does not have a smartphone, group chat culture affects them differently.

They may miss spontaneous shifts.

They may hear jokes later.

They may need clarification.

They may ask more questions.

That can feel tiring.

It can also build resilience — if supported well.

The difference lies in framing.

If your child believes delay equals deficiency, confidence drops.

If your child understands delay as preparation, steadiness grows.

Tone matters.

Confidence matters.

Parental framing matters.

A Small Scenario

Imagine this:

A group chat lights up at 8:30 p.m.

"Math test is canceled."

"Seriously?"

"Yeah, teacher posted it."

Ten children relax.

One child without access studies another hour.

The next morning, the rumor is false.

No one is harmed.

But emotionally, that child experienced being outside the flow.

Neither scenario is catastrophic.

But repeated micro-moments accumulate.

Accumulation shapes perception.

Perception shapes identity.

Emotional Readiness for Group Chats

Before entering group chat environments, children benefit from certain capacities.

They need to tolerate being ignored without spiraling.

They need to resist responding impulsively.

They need to step away from conflict.

They need to accept missing some things.

They need to sleep without compulsively checking.

These are not age-based skills.

They are regulation-based skills.

When these capacities exist, group chats become coordination tools.

Without them, group chats become emotional triggers.

Digital Status Mirrors Offline Status

Group chats do not create social hierarchy from nothing.

They amplify what already exists.

If your child feels secure offline, digital interaction tends to be lighter.

If your child feels uncertain offline, digital interaction often intensifies that uncertainty.

Technology magnifies.

It rarely repairs.

Parents sometimes hope access will elevate social standing.

Sometimes it does briefly.

But deeper belonging still depends on personality, kindness, shared experience, and mutual respect.

The chat may coordinate friendship.

It does not sustain it.

The Parent's Role

You cannot control group chat dynamics.

But you can prepare your child for them.

You can normalize not being included every time.

You can discuss tone and misunderstanding.

You can role-play responses to teasing.

You can teach that stepping away is strength, not weakness.

You can emphasize that digital presence does not define worth.

Curiosity works better than surveillance.

"How did that feel?"

"What did you want to say?"

"What stopped you?"

Conversation builds awareness.

Awareness builds regulation.

Regulation changes digital experience.

The Bigger Question

Group chats are not inherently harmful.

They are accelerators.

They accelerate inclusion.

They accelerate exclusion.

They accelerate humor.

They accelerate conflict.

Acceleration without maturity creates instability.

Acceleration with maturity builds skill.

Your child will eventually enter this environment.

The question is with what internal equipment.

The more stable the foundation, the less destabilizing the acceleration.

That foundation is built before entry.

And that is where timing matters.

5

Will My Child Lose Their Friends?

This is the question parents rarely say out loud — but think constantly.

If I delay a smartphone, will my child lose their friends?

Will invitations stop?

Will they drift to the edge of the group?

Will friendships reorganize quietly without them?

The fear is not about the device.

It is about loneliness.

And loneliness in childhood feels enormous.

Many parents remember their own middle school years.

The cafeteria tables.

The subtle hierarchies.

The birthday party you heard about afterward.

The sleepover everyone else attended.

Now imagine those moments unfolding in real time — visible on a screen.

Of course parents worry.

But here is something important:

A smartphone does not guarantee inclusion.

And the absence of one does not automatically cause exclusion.

Friendship is built on more than bandwidth.

What Actually Sustains Friendship

Strip away technology, and enduring friendships between ages nine and fourteen are sustained by:

Shared experience.

Shared humor.

Reliability.

Emotional safety.

Consistency.

Presence.

Phones coordinate friendship.

They do not create it.

A child who shows up in person — who listens, participates, and contributes — builds social capital that extends beyond digital access.

Digital presence can amplify connection.

But connection built only on digital interaction is often shallow.

Missing Messages vs. Missing Meaning

One of the biggest misunderstandings in this debate is the difference between missing messages and missing meaning.

Your child may miss a late-night joke.

They may miss a spontaneous suggestion.

They may hear about something the next morning instead of instantly.

But missing a message is not the same as missing belonging.

If your child still laughs at the story the next day, still participates in shared experiences, still feels welcomed face-to-face — the friendship is intact.

Children are more adaptable than adults assume.

Peers adjust.

Plans are repeated.

Stories are retold.

The digital world moves fast.

Real-world connection anchors friendship.

The Confidence Variable

The strongest predictor of sustained friendship is not smartphone ownership.

It is confidence.

Confident children initiate.

They ask directly.

They clarify plans.

They show up.

They recover from minor awkwardness.

An insecure child with a phone may still feel excluded.

A grounded child without one may thrive.

Technology amplifies personality.

It does not replace it.

The Transitional Phase

There may be a middle phase — and it is important to acknowledge it honestly.

When most peers receive smartphones, your child may feel different.

There may be moments of embarrassment.

Moments of frustration.

Moments of comparison.

This does not mean your strategy is failing.

It means your child is practicing being slightly outside the dominant current.

That practice can build resilience.

But it requires parental steadiness.

If you panic, your child absorbs that panic.

If you hold the line calmly, your child learns that discomfort is survivable.

The Role of Initiative

Children without smartphones often develop a subtle strength.

They learn to ask directly.

"What time is practice again?"

"Are we meeting at four?"

"Can you tell me in person tomorrow?"

Direct communication builds agency.

Agency builds confidence.

Confidence sustains friendship.

When children rely exclusively on passive updates, initiative weakens.

When they clarify in person, social skill strengthens.

These skills matter far beyond middle school.

The Myth of Constant Contact

Modern friendship appears constant.

Messages.

Threads.

Reactions.

But developmental psychology consistently shows that in-person interaction strengthens attachment far more effectively than digital exchange.

Shared physical experience creates stronger emotional encoding of belonging.

In simple terms:

Children remember how they felt with someone in person more than how many messages they exchanged.

If your child:

Plays on the same team.

Studies together.

Laughs face-to-face.

Walks home together.

The bond carries weight.

Digital communication supplements.

It rarely replaces.

When Friendships Drift

Sometimes, yes, a friendship may weaken during a delay period.

That can feel like confirmation of fear.

But pause.

Ask a harder question:

Was the friendship strong to begin with?

Some friendships are proximity-based.

Some are habit-based.

Some are depth-based.

Delaying smartphones can reveal the difference.

Shallow connections may fade.

Stronger ones often remain.

New ones may form around shared activities.

Clarity is not always loss.

Hosting and Physical Space

One of the most powerful ways to protect friendship without digital immersion is physical space.

Invite peers over.

Encourage study sessions.

Host small gatherings.

Children who spend time physically together strengthen bonds that extend beyond chat threads.

A home that feels welcoming increases your child's social gravity.

Friendship thrives where presence is consistent.

The Parent's Emotional Work

Often, anxiety about losing friends belongs as much to the parent as to the child.

Parents project their own memories.

Their own exclusions.

Their own regrets.

Your child's social world may not mirror yours.

Observe before assuming.

Ask before reacting.

Support before solving.

Confidence from you becomes confidence for them.

A Small Scene

Imagine a group decides in a chat to meet at the park.

Your child hears about it the next morning.

Instead of shrinking, they say:

"Hey, next time just tell me at school."

And the group adjusts.

That moment builds self-advocacy.

It communicates expectation without hostility.

Children often respect peers who communicate directly.

Not perfectly.

But more than we assume.

The Long View

You are not raising a twelve-year-old.

You are raising a future seventeen-year-old.

A future adult.

A person who will navigate digital culture independently.

The question is not:

How do I eliminate every moment of friction today?
The question is:
What skills will protect my child five years from now?
Skills like:
Initiating plans.
Recovering from awkwardness.
Tolerating mild exclusion.
Building one-on-one bonds.
These skills compound.
Compounding matters more than convenience.

When to Reconsider

Delay should not be rigid.
If your child shows:
Persistent isolation.
Rising anxiety.
Withdrawal from activities.
Consistent mood decline.
Reassess.
Not because of pressure.
Because well-being matters.
Every child's temperament is different.
Flexibility is strength.

The Real Question

Instead of asking:
Will my child lose their friends?
Ask:
What kind of friendships do I want my child to build?
Fast and constant?
Or steady and resilient?

Technology shapes the container.

Character shapes the connection.

If your child is kind, engaged, present, and supported — friendship will find them.

Not perfectly.

Not without moments of discomfort.

But authentically.

And authentic belonging is stronger than digital access alone.

6

Friction Is Not Isolation

One of the most important distinctions a parent can learn in the smartphone conversation is this:

Friction is not isolation.

Those two experiences feel similar in the moment.

Both involve discomfort.

Both involve being slightly outside the flow.

But they are fundamentally different.

Responding as if they are the same can distort your decision.

What Isolation Actually Looks Like

Isolation is sustained exclusion.

It looks like:

No invitations.

No inclusion in shared activities.

No one making eye contact at lunch.

No shared laughter.

No emotional connection.

Isolation is relational absence.

It is not about missed information.

It is about missing relationship.

When a child is isolated, the problem is not technology timing.
It is the social ecosystem itself.
And that requires intervention.

What Friction Looks Like

Friction is inconvenience.
It looks like:
"Wait, what time was practice again?"
"I didn't see that message."
"Can you tell me tomorrow?"
It may involve:
Hearing about a joke after it happened.
Missing a spontaneous plan.
Feeling half a beat behind.
Friction feels uncomfortable.
But discomfort is not damage.
Friction builds capacity when navigated calmly.
At lunch, everyone is laughing.
"I can't believe you said that."
"You saw it, right?"
He shakes his head.
They recap it for him.
It takes thirty seconds.
He laughs with them.
The moment passes.
It wasn't catastrophic.
Just slightly out of sync.

Why Parents Collapse the Two

Parents collapse friction into isolation because we fast-forward.

We imagine:

Missed message →

Missed joke →

Missed invitation →

Social drift →

Long-term loneliness.

But childhood is rarely that linear.

Children renegotiate social dynamics daily.

Plans repeat.

Stories are retold.

Friend groups shift constantly.

The social world of preteens is fluid, not fixed.

A single moment rarely determines trajectory.

The Brain's Threat Detection System

When a child experiences social friction, their brain reacts.

During pre-adolescence, threat detection systems are highly sensitive to peer evaluation.

A missed invitation can feel larger than it objectively is.

A delayed response can feel like rejection.

The emotional reaction is real.

But the meaning assigned to it is not always accurate.

If parents interpret every moment of friction as social threat, the child learns that discomfort equals danger.

That association increases anxiety.

If parents frame friction as navigable, the child learns resilience.

Framing matters.

A Small Scenario

Imagine this:

A group chat forms a last-minute plan to get ice cream.

Your child hears about it later.

They feel briefly disappointed.

That is friction.

Now imagine:

Your child repeatedly sees photos of gatherings they were never invited to.

They sit alone at lunch consistently.

No one includes them in shared activity.

That is isolation.

These experiences require different responses.

Friction requires coaching.

Isolation requires intervention.

Confusing them can create unnecessary urgency.

The Skill Hidden Inside Friction

Friction creates opportunity.

It forces children to:

Ask directly.

Clarify details.

Initiate plans.

Develop patience.

Tolerate mild embarrassment.

These micro-skills are not glamorous.

But they build social agency.

Children who must advocate for clarity become more comfortable speaking up.

Children who tolerate manageable discomfort build emotional strength.

Shielding children from all friction can unintentionally weaken capacity.

Capacity grows through manageable challenge.

The Cultural Pressure to Eliminate Discomfort

Modern parenting culture often equates discomfort with harm.
We want smoothness.
We want efficiency.
We want seamless experiences.
But seamless childhood is not realistic.
Social development has always involved awkwardness.
The difference now is visibility.
Digital platforms make small moments visible.
Visibility intensifies reaction.
But visibility does not automatically equal severity.
Learning to interpret visibility accurately is part of digital maturity.

When Friction Builds Confidence

Children who navigate friction successfully often develop subtle confidence.
They learn:
I can handle being slightly different.
I can recover from mild embarrassment.
I can ask for what I need.
I can tolerate missing something.
That confidence compounds.
When they eventually enter digital spaces more fully, they are less reactive.
Less desperate for reassurance.
Less likely to equate silence with rejection.
Friction becomes training.

The Parent's Tone

The way you respond to friction shapes how your child interprets it.
If you respond with:
"This is why you need a phone."

The message becomes:

Without access, you are vulnerable.

If you respond with:

"That's frustrating. What can you do next time?"

The message becomes:

You have tools.

That shift strengthens agency.

Agency reduces anxiety.

The Long-Term Advantage of Slight Asymmetry

Being slightly out of sync socially is not inherently harmful.

In fact, mild asymmetry can build perspective.

Children who are not fully immersed sometimes:

Observe more.

Listen more.

Engage more intentionally.

They are not constantly reacting to digital stimuli.

They develop parallel interests.

They invest in offline hobbies.

Those investments diversify identity.

When identity is diversified, social fluctuations feel less threatening.

The Risk of Over-Correction

In the effort to eliminate friction, some parents introduce smartphones earlier than necessary.

The logic is understandable:

If access reduces discomfort, access must be the solution.

But access often shifts the discomfort.

Instead of missing messages, the child may:

Feel pressure to respond quickly.

Monitor reactions obsessively.

Experience comparison more intensely.

The friction does not disappear.

It changes form.

The question becomes:

Which form builds more long-term capacity?

Building Tolerance for Small Misses

You can help your child build tolerance for friction by normalizing it.

"It's okay to miss something."

"Plans change."

"You can ask tomorrow."

These phrases seem small.

But repetition shapes narrative.

If your child hears that minor social misses are survivable, their nervous system relaxes.

Relaxation reduces reactivity.

Reduced reactivity increases confidence.

The Stability Equation

Isolation undermines stability.

Friction builds it.

Isolation removes opportunity.

Friction invites growth.

Your role is not to eliminate all discomfort.

It is to distinguish between discomfort and harm.

When you respond proportionally, your child learns proportional thinking.

Proportional thinking is a core component of emotional maturity.

The Deeper Question

When evaluating whether to introduce a smartphone, ask:

Is my child experiencing sustained exclusion?

Or occasional inconvenience?

If it is sustained exclusion, the phone may not be the primary issue.

If it is occasional inconvenience, capacity-building may be more powerful than immediate access.

Clarity reduces urgency.

Urgency often drives premature decisions.

Steadiness Over Speed

Childhood has always involved moments of being slightly outside the circle.

What builds resilience is not avoiding those moments.

It is navigating them with support.

Friction, handled calmly, strengthens internal footing.

Isolation, ignored, weakens it.

Knowing the difference protects your child far more effectively than reacting quickly.

The goal is not seamless childhood.

It is stable development.

And stable development often grows through manageable friction.

7

How to Delay Without Losing Connection

Delaying a smartphone is not the hardest part.

Losing connection is the fear.

When parents hesitate, it is rarely because they dislike technology.

It is because they are trying to protect two things at once:

Their child's development.

Their child's belonging.

If delay feels like social risk, it becomes unsustainable.

So the real question becomes:

How do you delay without shrinking your child's social world?

The answer is not control.

It is intentional substitution.

Connection Does Not Require Constant Access

One of the quiet myths of modern childhood is that friendship requires constant digital presence.

It does not.

What sustains friendship is momentum:

Shared experiences.

Repeated proximity.

Mutual reliability.

Inside jokes built in person.

The mistake many families make when delaying a phone is assuming that the absence of digital coordination will automatically weaken bonds.

It only weakens bonds if nothing replaces it.

If delay is passive, friendships drift.

If delay is intentional, connection strengthens.

Increase Physical Proximity

Physical presence builds social gravity.

When your home becomes a gathering place, your child's social relevance increases.

Host study sessions.

Invite teammates over after practice.

Allow spontaneous drop-ins when possible.

Children who are consistently physically present in each other's lives build depth that extends beyond chat threads.

Shared space creates shared memory.

Shared memory creates loyalty.

Loyalty sustains friendship more than rapid response ever will.

Strengthen One-on-One Bonds

Group chats amplify social noise.

Lasting friendship often forms in smaller circles.

Encourage your child to invest in one-on-one time.

A walk after school.

A shared hobby.

A project built together.

One stable friendship often provides more emotional security than a large digital network.

Children who feel anchored in even one deep bond are less reactive to broader group fluctuations.

Depth reduces dependency on constant inclusion.

Teach Direct Communication

Digital culture rewards passive updating.

Delay requires active clarification.

Teach your child to say:

"What time exactly?"

"Can we decide before we leave school?"

"Let me know in person tomorrow."

Direct communication builds confidence.

Confidence increases social respect.

Peers often respond positively to clarity.

Children who speak up become socially memorable.

They are less likely to be overlooked.

Normalize Small Misses

Your child will miss something.

A joke.

A spontaneous change.

A late-night thread.

If every miss is framed as evidence of disadvantage, resentment grows.

If misses are framed as normal, tolerance builds.

Language matters.

"Sounds like that was chaotic."

"You can ask them about it tomorrow."

"You didn't miss much."

Calm framing reduces emotional intensity.

Intensity drives urgency.

Calm builds perspective.

Protect Sleep as a Social Strategy

Sleep is not just physical health.

It is social strength.

A well-rested child regulates emotion better.

Interprets tone more accurately.

Recovers from awkwardness faster.

When many peers are sleep-deprived due to late-night digital activity, your rested child may carry an invisible advantage.

They are clearer.

More stable.

Less reactive.

Stability attracts.

Expand Identity Beyond the Group

One of the greatest risks of early digital immersion is identity narrowing.

When a child's world revolves around one group chat, fluctuations feel catastrophic.

Encourage diversified identity.

Sports.

Music.

Debate.

Art.

Volunteer work.

Clubs.

When belonging exists in multiple environments, no single space defines self-worth.

Diversification reduces emotional fragility.

Fragility drives desperation.

Desperation strains friendship.

Model Calm Confidence

Children watch how you speak about delay.
    If you sound apologetic, they internalize deficiency.
    If you sound confident, they internalize steadiness.
    You do not need to criticize other families.
    You do not need to over-justify.
    You can simply say:
    "We're building skills first."
    Confidence without defensiveness communicates security.
    Security transfers.

Address Embarrassment Directly

Embarrassment is often the hidden emotion in smartphone delay.
    Your child may fear being the only one.
    Equip them with language.
    "We're waiting a bit."
    "My parents are slow about it."
    "It's coming later."
    Short. Neutral. Calm.
    Confidence reduces teasing.
    Teasing feeds on visible insecurity.

Keep Communication Open

Delay should never feel like secrecy.
    Invite conversation.
    Ask:
    "What feels hardest lately?"
    "Anything new happening in the group?"
    "How are you feeling about it now?"
    When children feel heard, they are less likely to escalate demands.

When they feel dismissed, they push harder.

Curiosity maintains connection inside your home.

Home stability protects external confidence.

Reevaluate Periodically

Delay is not permanent.

It is developmental.

Set informal checkpoints.

Middle school transitions.

New responsibilities.

Visible emotional growth.

When children see that timing connects to maturity — not arbitrary control — resentment decreases.

They understand the process.

Process builds trust.

Trust sustains relationship.

The Hidden Advantage of Delay

Children who learn to build friendship without constant digital reinforcement often develop subtle resilience.

They learn to:

Sit in mild discomfort.

Clarify directly.

Recover quickly.

Value depth over noise.

When they eventually receive smartphones, they enter with less hunger.

Less desperation.

Less fear of missing out.

They already know they can belong.

Belonging built without constant access is steadier when access arrives.

The Long View

Delaying without losing connection requires intention.

It requires presence.

It requires conversation.

It requires creating environments where your child's social life continues to grow.

But when done thoughtfully, delay does not shrink friendship.

It reshapes it.

From reactive to intentional.

From fast to steady.

From noise-driven to character-driven.

Connection does not depend on constant availability.

It depends on reliability, presence, and emotional safety.

Those qualities can be built long before a device enters your child's pocket.

And once built, they remain.

8

What "Ready" Actually Means

Most families do not struggle with whether their child will eventually receive a smartphone.

They struggle with when.

And the most common answer sounds reasonable:

"When they're ready."

But ready for what?

Ready is often treated like a feeling.

A sense.

An intuition.

One week your child seems mature.

The next week they dissolve because someone didn't respond quickly.

Readiness cannot be measured by age alone.

It cannot be measured by peer pressure.

It cannot be measured by how convincingly your child argues.

Readiness must be measured by capacity.

Capacity, Not Comparison

Cultural averages create artificial urgency.

"Sixth grade is normal."

"By seventh grade they need one."

"Eighth grade is too late."

These statements sound authoritative.

They are not developmental benchmarks.

Two twelve-year-olds can differ dramatically in emotional regulation, impulse control, and resilience.

Comparison is external.

Capacity is internal.

Internal strength predicts healthier digital integration far better than age.

Developmental neuroscience supports this. The prefrontal cortex — responsible for planning, inhibition, and impulse control — develops gradually through adolescence. Meanwhile, emotional and social sensitivity systems activate earlier.

That imbalance explains why a child can sound logical one moment and reactive the next.

Age does not equal regulation.

Capacity does.

The Four Dimensions of Readiness

True readiness has four components:

Emotional readiness.

Social readiness.

Cognitive readiness.

Behavioral readiness.

If one of these areas is significantly underdeveloped, the smartphone magnifies that weakness.

The device does not create instability.

It amplifies what already exists.

Emotional Readiness

Emotional readiness is the ability to experience discomfort without escalation.

A smartphone introduces:

Delayed responses.

Visible comparison.

Public mistakes.

Group chat dynamics.

Exclusion.

Overexposure.

Ask yourself:

When your child feels left out, what happens?

Do they reflect and recover?

Or do they spiral and ruminate?

When plans change, can they adapt?

Or do they react intensely?

Emotional readiness does not mean perfection.

It means recovery.

It means the ability to regulate emotion most of the time without external rescue.

Digital environments increase emotional input dramatically. The brain must filter more stimuli — more reactions, more comments, more feedback.

Regulation must be strong enough to absorb that load.

Social Readiness

Social readiness is the ability to navigate peer dynamics without collapsing or over-performing.

In group chats, tone is unclear.

Humor sharpens.

Hierarchy forms quickly.

Ask:

Can your child tolerate being ignored occasionally?

Can they disagree respectfully?

Can they resist joining teasing to protect their own status?

Can they leave a conversation when it becomes uncomfortable?

Social maturity involves restraint.

A smartphone provides publishing power.

Children who are still seeking constant validation may misuse that power.

Not maliciously.

But impulsively.

Adolescents are neurologically wired to value peer acceptance. That sensitivity is developmental — not weakness.

But it means social pressure in digital spaces feels amplified.

Readiness means the ability to withstand that amplification.

Cognitive Readiness

Cognitive readiness is the ability to understand permanence and consequence.

Screenshots exist.

Messages can be forwarded.

Digital footprints last.

Can your child grasp that something funny today may feel embarrassing later?

Do they think beyond the present moment?

Executive function — including foresight and inhibitory control — continues strengthening into mid-adolescence.

Cognitive readiness does not require adult-level foresight.

But it requires awareness.

Without awareness, digital missteps compound quickly.

Behavioral Readiness

Behavioral readiness is often the clearest indicator.

Can your child manage:

Homework without constant reminders?

Bedtime with reasonable consistency?

Shared device limits responsibly?

Chores without negotiation every time?

Behavior reveals readiness more clearly than promises.

If self-regulation is inconsistent in low-stakes environments, unlimited digital access will not improve it.

Digital environments increase cognitive load — more decisions, more temptations, more distractions.

Structure outside digital life predicts structure inside digital life.

Digital Readiness Ladder

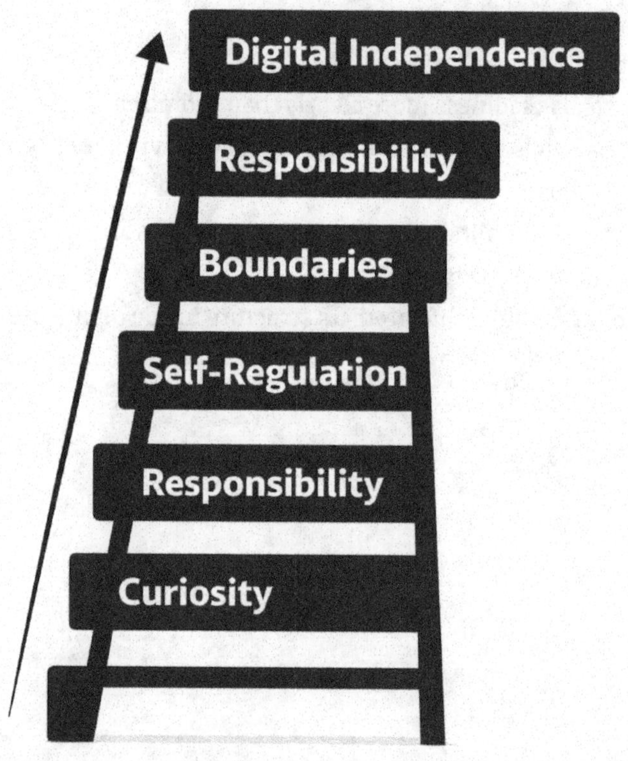

The Illusion of Desire

Many children want smartphones intensely.

Desire is not evidence of readiness.

Desire is evidence of social awareness.

Children want to belong.

They want autonomy.

They want parity with peers.

Those desires are normal.

But readiness is not measured by how strongly something is wanted.

It is measured by how well it can be handled.

The "I'll Know When I See It" Trap

Some parents wait for a vague sense of maturity.

Intuition matters.

But structure protects clarity.

Instead of waiting for a feeling, establish benchmarks.

Can your child go one week without arguing about screen limits?

Can they resolve a minor peer conflict without adult intervention?

Can they tolerate delayed gratification?

Can they demonstrate emotional recovery after disappointment?

Self-regulation strengthens through practice and feedback — not assumption.

Benchmarks turn readiness into process.

Process reduces conflict.

When children see what maturity looks like, they can work toward it.

Without benchmarks, the debate becomes endless.

Expand or Shrink?

Before introducing a smartphone, ask one decisive question:
Will this expand my child's world — or shrink it?
Expansion looks like:
Greater responsibility.
Increased independence.
Improved coordination.
Opportunity growth.
Shrinking looks like:
More comparison.
More distraction.
Increased anxiety.
Reduced in-person engagement.
Be honest.
If the likely impact is shrinking, it may not be time.

Early Introduction vs. Gradual Integration

Some families introduce smartphones fully.
Others introduce them gradually.
Gradual integration may include:
Shared device use.
A basic phone first.
Limited smartphone access.
Monitored expansion.
Gradual exposure allows capacity to grow alongside access.
Sudden unlimited access demands capacity immediately.
The brain adapts to environments.
A stepped approach allows regulatory systems to strengthen as exposure increases.

When Delay Becomes Counterproductive

It is important to acknowledge the opposite risk.

Excessive delay without communication can create secrecy.

Children may borrow friends' devices.

Create hidden accounts.

Hide usage.

Feel infantilized.

Readiness is not permanent delay.

It is calibrated timing.

The goal is confident integration — not prolonged restriction.

Temperament Matters

Every child is different.

Anxious children may need more emotional scaffolding.

Highly impulsive children may need more structure.

Socially dominant children may tolerate delay more easily.

Introverted children may process digital exposure differently than extroverted ones.

Temperament influences how stimulation is processed.

Age-based rules ignore individual differences.

Individual awareness strengthens timing decisions.

The Maturity Gap

Digital platforms are engineered for engagement.

Notifications trigger reward pathways.

Algorithms prioritize emotionally charged content.

Even adults struggle with impulse control in these environments.

Children require stronger guardrails.

If internal regulation precedes immersion, the environment feels manageable.

If immersion precedes regulation, overwhelm increases.
The maturity gap is not moral failure.
It is developmental reality.

The Long-Term Goal

Eventually, most children will receive smartphones.
When that day comes, it should feel like transition — not surrender.
"You've built the skills for this."
That sentence reframes the device.
It becomes a tool.
Not a lifeline.
Not a status symbol.
Not a rescue from exclusion.
A tool.
Tools require training.
Training requires time.
Time requires patience.
Patience builds maturity.

The Core Standard

Readiness is not about fitting in.
It is about functioning well inside complexity.
If your child can:
Handle delayed responses.
Tolerate minor exclusion.
Manage emotion consistently.
Respect boundaries.
Think beyond the present moment.
Integration is likely smoother.
If not, preparation may still be underway.
There is courage in waiting.

There is also courage in granting access.

The difference is clarity.

And clarity grows when readiness is defined by capacity — not comparison.

9

The Digital Maturity Checklist

Parents often ask for something simple.

"Just tell me how to know."

How do I know if my child is ready?

How do I measure something as abstract as maturity?

The problem is not lack of desire.

It is lack of clarity.

If readiness remains vague, decisions become reactive.

If readiness becomes visible, decisions become calm.

This chapter is not about rigid standards.

It is about observing patterns.

Because maturity is not a moment.

It is consistency over time.

Emotional Stability Under Mild Pressure

One of the clearest indicators of digital maturity is how your child handles minor emotional stress.

Not major crises.

Minor disappointments.

A friend forgets to include them.

A plan changes.

Someone does not respond immediately.

Do they:

Pause and process?

Or escalate quickly?

Digital environments amplify minor stressors.

If your child can already navigate mild frustration without unraveling, they are building the foundation necessary for online interaction.

If minor stress leads to extended rumination or explosive reaction, more strengthening may be needed.

Tolerance for Delayed Gratification

Smartphones reward immediacy.

Instant replies.

Instant reactions.

Instant novelty.

Before introducing that system, ask:

Can your child wait?

Can they tolerate not knowing something immediately?

Can they delay gratification in other areas of life?

Delayed gratification predicts self-regulation.

Self-regulation predicts healthier digital use.

This is not about perfection.

It is about trend.

Does your child usually wait — or usually demand?

Patterns reveal readiness.

Ownership of Mistakes

Digital life contains permanence.

Children will misjudge tone.

Misinterpret humor.

Post impulsively.

The question is not whether mistakes will happen.

The question is how they are handled.

When your child makes a mistake now, what happens?

Do they deflect responsibility?

Blame others?

Or acknowledge and repair?

Repair capacity is crucial in digital spaces.

Without it, missteps compound.

With it, recovery becomes possible.

Respect for Boundaries

Before introducing a device that requires self-regulation, examine existing limits.

Does your child respect screen rules on shared devices?

Do they negotiate endlessly?

Do they attempt to circumvent restrictions?

If current limits require constant enforcement, full smartphone access may amplify conflict.

Readiness includes internalizing boundaries — not just complying when monitored.

Sleep Discipline

Sleep may seem unrelated.

It is not.

If your child already struggles to separate from devices at night, a smartphone increases that struggle.

Ask yourself:

Can they stop an activity without escalating?

Can they wind down without digital input?

Can they protect their own rest?

Emotional regulation deteriorates quickly under sleep deprivation.

Digital maturity includes the ability to disengage.

Conflict Navigation Without Adult Rescue

Before entering group chats and social media, children benefit from practicing conflict repair in real life.

When conflict arises at school:

Do they attempt resolution?

Or immediately seek adult intervention?

Digital conflicts move quickly.

Screenshots spread.

Side conversations form.

Rumors accelerate.

If your child has little experience resolving interpersonal tension independently, online conflict may feel overwhelming.

Experience builds resilience.

Self-Generated Engagement

Can your child occupy themselves without constant external stimulation?

Boredom tolerance correlates strongly with creativity and emotional flexibility.

If silence feels intolerable, digital immersion may become coping rather than tool.

Children who can generate their own engagement are less likely to depend on notifications for stimulation.

Perspective After Disappointment

When something goes wrong socially, how long does it dominate your child's mood?

Minutes?

Hours?

Days?

Digital life compresses social cycles.

Disappointments happen faster and more frequently.

Recovery speed matters.

A child who rebounds reasonably quickly from mild social setbacks is better equipped to manage digital fluctuations.

Desire vs. Capacity

It is essential to separate desire from capacity.

Your child may argue convincingly.

They may insist they are responsible.

They may point to peers who already have devices.

None of that measures regulation.

Capacity shows up in daily habits.

Consistency.

Reaction patterns.

Recovery speed.

Behavior reveals more than argument.

A Quiet Self-Assessment

Instead of asking your child to defend their readiness, observe quietly.

For several weeks, pay attention to:

How they respond to minor frustration.

How they handle waiting.

How they manage current screen limits.

How they repair mistakes.

How they recover emotionally.

Patterns provide clarity.

Clarity reduces reactive decision-making.

When Capacity Aligns

When you begin to notice that your child:

Handles disappointment with increasing steadiness.

Accepts boundaries with less resistance.

Resolves small conflicts independently.

Manages time more responsibly.

Recovers from embarrassment more quickly.

Readiness may be emerging.

It will not be dramatic.

It will be subtle.

But consistent.

Consistency signals capacity.

Capacity signals timing.

The Role of Trust

Trust is mutual.

Your child must trust that you are not delaying arbitrarily.

You must trust that they can handle expanded responsibility.

When readiness is discussed openly — not as punishment but as progression — trust strengthens.

"You're building toward this."

That framing transforms the phone from status symbol to milestone.

Milestones feel earned.

Earned milestones feel respected.

Respect reduces rebellion.

Avoid Public Benchmarks

One common mistake is announcing readiness criteria in an adversarial tone.

"You can't have one until you prove yourself."

That framing invites power struggle.

Instead, keep benchmarks developmental.

"We want to see more consistency with bedtime."

"We want to see you handling frustration calmly."

Quiet observation often works better than declared requirements.

The goal is growth, not performance.

The Final Question

Before introducing a smartphone, ask yourself:

If this device enters my child's life tomorrow, am I confident they can use it without it using them?

That question cuts through noise.

You do not need guarantees.

You need reasonable confidence.

If that confidence is absent, more preparation may serve better than acceleration.

If it is present, integration can be thoughtful.

Readiness is not about control.

It is about timing strength.

When timing aligns with capacity, transition becomes smoother.

When timing outruns capacity, friction increases.

Digital maturity is not an age.

It is a pattern.

And patterns reveal themselves quietly — if you are paying attention.

10

When to Say Yes

For many parents, delay feels easier than permission.

Waiting feels protective.

Saying yes feels irreversible.

Delay feels like control.

Permission feels like exposure.

But at some point, the conversation shifts.

Not because pressure wins.

Not because comparison exhausts you.

Not because you are tired of defending your reasoning.

But because readiness becomes visible.

And when readiness is visible, hesitation begins to feel unnecessary.

The goal of delay is not permanent resistance.

It is prepared transition.

So when do you say yes?

Not when your child argues best.

Not when "everyone else" reaches a tipping point.

Not when you are simply tired of the debate.

You say yes when capacity matches complexity.

The Moment Feels Different

When readiness is real, the tone changes.

Desperation fades.

Frustration softens.

Urgency disappears.

Your child sounds steady instead of frantic.

Curious instead of defensive.

Focused on function instead of status.

The device is no longer positioned as rescue.

It becomes responsibility.

That difference matters.

What Developmental Readiness Actually Means

From a developmental standpoint, this shift makes sense.

The prefrontal cortex — responsible for impulse control, planning, and emotional regulation — continues developing into the mid-twenties. In early adolescence, emotional systems are highly active while regulatory systems are still strengthening.

That imbalance is normal.

It explains why middle schoolers can understand consequences in theory but struggle to apply them under social pressure.

Readiness is not perfection.

It is increasing regulation.

You are watching for patterns:

Reduced impulsivity.

Improved emotional recovery.

Greater follow-through.

Increased tolerance for boredom.

Less reactivity to peer comparison.

You are not waiting for full maturity.

You are waiting for functional capacity.

Expansion, Not Escape

The right time to say yes often arrives when the smartphone will expand your child's world — not stabilize it.

If the phone is meant to:

Coordinate increasing responsibilities.

Support academic independence.

Facilitate structured activities.

Strengthen existing friendships.

Then it is a tool.

If the phone is meant to:

Fix insecurity.

Solve exclusion.

Calm anxiety.

Repair social instability.

Then it becomes a crutch.

Tools empower.

Crutches compensate.

The difference is intention.

The Calm Test

Before saying yes, imagine the device arriving.

Does your nervous system feel settled?

Or tight?

If you feel uneasy — not from fear, but from premature timing — listen to that signal.

Parent intuition is not superstition.

It is pattern recognition.

You have watched your child navigate disappointment, conflict, embarrassment, impulse, comparison.

If those patterns show steadiness, integration is likely smoother.

If volatility remains frequent, more time may serve better.

WHEN IS MY CHILD READY?

USE THIS DECISION FLOWCHART BEFORE GIVING YOUR CHILD A SMARTPHONE

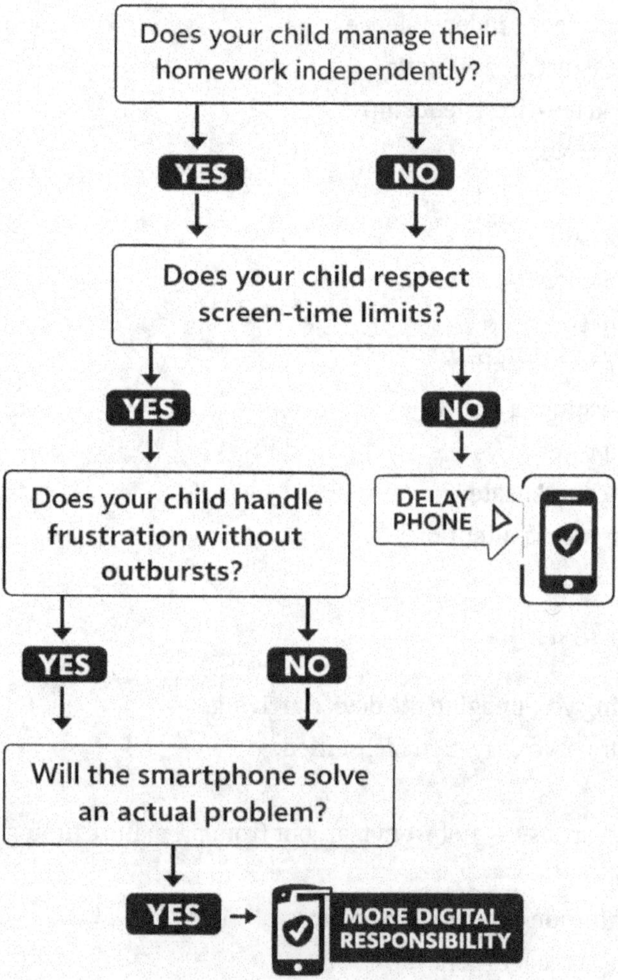

Does your child manage their homework independently?

- **YES**
- **NO**

Does your child respect screen-time limits?

- **YES**
- **NO**

DELAY PHONE

Does your child handle frustration without outbursts?

- **YES**
- **NO**

Will the smartphone solve an actual problem?

YES → **MORE DIGITAL RESPONSIBILITY**

Executive Function Matters

Executive function — the ability to plan, prioritize, inhibit impulses, and manage attention — develops gradually through adolescence.

Smartphones increase demands on executive function.

They introduce:

Constant notifications.

Social comparison.

Instant emotional feedback.

Unlimited stimulation.

A child who cannot yet manage homework without reminders will struggle more — not less — when that device is added.

But a child who increasingly self-corrects, plans ahead, and tolerates delayed gratification is building the internal structure required for digital independence.

You are not asking:

"Are they old enough?"

You are asking:

"Are they regulated enough?"

Responsibility Before Privilege

When you say yes, frame the decision around growth.

"This is expansion."

"You've shown us you can handle more."

"You've built the skills for this."

Language shapes identity.

If the phone is introduced as reward for pressure, pressure continues.

If it is introduced as recognition of maturity, maturity strengthens.

Children rise toward how we frame them.

Establish Purpose

Before the device arrives, clarify purpose.
Why now?
Is your child entering a new school?
Traveling independently?
Managing a busier schedule?
Participating in more coordinated activities?
Greater responsibility justifies greater access.
Purpose grounds permission.
Without purpose, devices drift toward entertainment and comparison.
With purpose, structure forms naturally.

A Gradual Yes

Saying yes does not require total immersion.
Integration can be phased:
Limited app access.
No social media initially.
Restricted group chats.
No overnight charging in bedrooms.
Gradual expansion mirrors developmental progression.
Sudden unlimited access overwhelms.
Gradual integration builds capacity alongside exposure.
Growth remains aligned with readiness.

The First Months Matter

The initial weeks after introduction set patterns.

Research on habit formation shows that early routines strongly influence long-term behavior. When norms are clear from the beginning — charging outside bedrooms, no devices during homework blocks, no late-night scrolling — those habits stabilize faster than parents expect.

Consistency matters more than strictness.

Calm repetition builds habit.

Habit shapes identity.

If usage becomes constant immediately, recalibration becomes harder.

If structure is clear, adjustment is smoother.

Watch for Shifts

After saying yes, observe.

Not obsessively.

But attentively.

Does your child remain engaged offline?

Are mood patterns stable?

Is sleep protected?

Sleep is not a small detail.

Even modest reductions in sleep during adolescence correlate with increased irritability, reduced attention, and heightened emotional reactivity. Blue light exposure late at night can delay melatonin release, making it harder for developing brains to settle.

Sleep stability is often the first indicator of digital imbalance.

If instability rises sharply, recalibrate.

Integration is adjustable.

Flexibility is strength.

Avoid All-or-Nothing Thinking

Some families treat smartphones as binary.

Total freedom.

Total prohibition.

Both extremes create tension.

The goal is neither control nor surrender.

The goal is guided independence.

Independence grows gradually.

Permission should mirror growth.

A Different Kind of Confidence

When the timing is right, saying yes does not feel like loss of control.
It feels like alignment.
You are not giving in.
You are acknowledging growth.
Permission given from calm authority builds respect.
Permission given from exhaustion builds entitlement.
The tone you carry into the transition shapes what follows.

The Long View

Eventually, your child will navigate digital spaces without your supervision.
You are not preparing them to live under restriction.
You are preparing them to live with discernment.
When you say yes at the right time, the device does not feel like forbidden fruit.
It feels normal.
Integrated.
Manageable.
He opens the box slowly.
Not frantic.
Not triumphant.
Just steady.
You review the agreement together.
He nods.
That night, he plugs it in outside his room without being reminded.
No celebration.
No announcement.
Just readiness meeting responsibility.
That is the goal.

Not early.
Not late.
Aligned.
When capacity and complexity meet, integration stabilizes.
That is when you say yes.

11

A Gradual Release Plan

When families think about smartphones, they often imagine a single moment.

A birthday.

A holiday.

A milestone.

The device is wrapped.

Opened.

Activated.

And just like that, childhood shifts.

But integration does not have to be abrupt.

It can be staged.

Gradual release protects both development and relationship.

Because the real goal is not ownership.

It is self-regulation.

And self-regulation grows best in layers.

Stage One: Shared Access

Before a smartphone becomes personal, access can be shared.

A family device used for specific purposes:

Texting a teammate about practice.

Calling a friend under supervision.

Limited, purposeful interaction.

This stage accomplishes something subtle but important.

It separates communication from possession.

Your child begins learning how digital interaction feels — without the emotional weight of ownership.

They experience group coordination.

They observe tone.

They encounter minor social ambiguity.

But with guardrails.

This stage builds familiarity without immersion.

It lowers novelty before responsibility expands.

Stage Two: A Basic Phone

For some families, the next step is not a smartphone.

It is a basic phone.

Calls.

Texts.

No social media.

No endless scroll.

This phase supports logistical independence.

Your child can coordinate plans.

You can reach them directly.

But the environment remains contained.

A basic phone introduces responsibility without comparison-driven platforms.

It builds accountability:

Charging the phone.

Answering responsibly.

Managing communication without entertainment layered on top.

Not every family chooses this path.

But for many, it provides a stabilizing bridge.

Stage Three: Limited Smartphone Access

When the smartphone arrives, structure should already exist.
Before activation, establish expectations calmly.
Where will the phone sleep?
How will apps be chosen?
What happens when limits are exceeded?
Clarity reduces conflict.
Ambiguity invites negotiation.
Early boundaries often include:
No overnight bedroom charging.
No social media initially.
Limited group chat inclusion.
Defined usage windows rather than open access.
This stage should feel structured, not oppressive.
The goal is to prevent immediate overexposure.
Children adapt to early norms quickly.
If limits are clear from day one, they feel normal.
If limits are imposed after patterns form, resistance increases.

The First Emotional Spike

When smartphones are introduced, there is often a short-term spike in intensity.
Excitement.
Increased checking.
Heightened sensitivity to notifications.
This is normal.
Novelty activates reward pathways.
Your role is not to eliminate excitement.
It is to steady it.
Stay consistent.
Stay calm.

Reinforce limits without escalation.

Patterns stabilize over weeks, not days.

Stage Four: Expanding Autonomy

As regulation proves consistent, autonomy can expand.

More app access.

Longer usage windows.

Greater privacy.

Autonomy should mirror demonstrated maturity.

If your child consistently protects sleep, respects limits, and navigates minor digital friction calmly, trust grows.

Trust invites expansion.

Expansion without trust creates instability.

Gradual autonomy builds confidence — both yours and theirs.

Transparency Without Surveillance

One of the hardest tensions parents navigate is privacy.

Children need space.

Parents need awareness.

Early in integration, transparency matters more than privacy.

Not because of mistrust.

Because of training.

You might say:

"For now, we'll check in occasionally."

"We want to help you build good habits."

As maturity stabilizes, surveillance decreases.

Trust deepens.

Privacy expands.

Privacy given too early feels like abandonment.

Privacy earned feels empowering.

Reset Is Not Failure

There may be moments when limits need tightening.

Late-night use.

Conflict escalation.

Emotional reactivity increasing.

A reset does not mean the plan failed.

It means adjustment is needed.

Speak calmly:

"We need to recalibrate."

Avoid shaming language.

The goal is growth, not punishment.

When children understand that boundaries are fluid based on behavior, they begin linking freedom to responsibility.

That linkage is powerful.

Protect Sleep as Non-Negotiable

Across all stages, sleep must remain protected.

Charging outside the bedroom.

Digital cut-off times.

Clear evening routines.

Sleep is emotional armor.

Without it, even mature children destabilize.

This boundary should be firm.

Not punitive.

Protective.

Family Culture Matters

Gradual release works best inside consistent family culture.

If parents scroll constantly, rules feel hypocritical.

If devices dominate dinner, boundaries feel arbitrary.

Modeling matters.
Children internalize what they observe.
A household that values presence reduces digital overreach naturally.
Structure feels shared, not imposed.

Avoid the Cliff

The most destabilizing approach is the cliff.
Total restriction followed by total access.
No scaffolding.
No training.
No progressive autonomy.
Children who go from zero to unlimited immersion experience a sharp learning curve.
Steeper curves increase risk.
Gradual slopes build confidence.

SCREEN-TIME ZONE MODEL

Create Healthy Boundaries for Tech Use

RED ZONE

NO DEVICES ALLOWED

- Meals & Family Time
- Bedrooms (Night)
- School Hours
- Before Bedtime
- Sensitive Conversations

YELLOW ZONE

SUPERVISED USE

- Homework Time
- Video Calls
- Educational Apps
- Public Places
- Time Limit. 30–60 min/day

GREEN ZONE

INDEPENDENT USE

- After Responsibilities Met
- With Parental Consent
- Time Limit Set
- Respect & Balance
- Open Communication

FAMILY RULES

| Respect Time Limits | No Secrets | Charge Outside Bedroom | Review Weekly |

Balance → Responsibility → Trust

The Goal of Gradual Release

Gradual release transforms the smartphone from status symbol into developmental milestone.

It shifts the narrative from:

"I finally got one."

To:

"I'm learning to manage one."

That difference shapes identity.

One reinforces entitlement.

The other reinforces responsibility.

When responsibility precedes freedom, freedom stabilizes.

The Long-Term Aim

Eventually, your child will manage digital life independently.

You are not building lifelong restriction.

You are building lifelong regulation.

Regulation grows through repetition.

Repetition requires structure.

Structure requires patience.

Gradual release is not slower parenting.

It is strategic parenting.

Complexity should match capacity.

When capacity grows, complexity can expand.

That alignment protects both development and relationship.

And relationship matters more than any device.

12

If You Already Gave Them a Smartphone

By the time many parents begin asking harder questions about smartphones, the device is already in their child's hand.

It may have been:

A birthday gift.

A holiday surprise.

A response to peer pressure.

A logistical necessity.

A moment of exhaustion.

Or simply a moment that felt reasonable at the time.

And now, weeks or months later, something feels unsettled.

Sleep is lighter.

Mood feels sharper.

Arguments increase.

Checking becomes constant.

Your child seems both connected and distracted at the same time.

If this is your reality, pause.

You did not ruin your child's development.

You are not behind.

You are not powerless.

Integration is adjustable.

The story does not end at "yes."

A Group Chat Moment

A mother described the shift this way.

Her son received a phone at the start of middle school. At first, it felt manageable. He texted about homework. Coordinated soccer practice. Shared jokes.

Then one evening, he came downstairs unusually quiet.

"What's wrong?" she asked.

"Nothing," he said.

Later that night, notification after notification sounded from his room. Laughter. Then silence. Then more notifications.

The next morning, he was irritable. Distracted. Preoccupied.

Eventually he admitted: someone had posted a photo from school and a group chat erupted. Not about him — but about someone else. He didn't want to participate. But he didn't want to be absent either.

"I just didn't know when to stop reading it," he said.

That sentence captures the heart of digital recalibration.

Not crisis.

But overload.

The Myth of No Return

Many parents assume that once a smartphone enters a child's life, boundaries can only move in one direction — toward more freedom.

This is not true.

Access can be recalibrated.

Privileges can be structured.

Usage can be redesigned.

Recalibration is not failure.

It is leadership.

Children test environments.

Parents shape them.

When something feels unstable, it is appropriate to adjust.

Not abruptly.

Not angrily.

But clearly.

Why Overuse Escalates Quickly

Digital platforms are designed around reward cycles.

Notifications trigger small dopamine releases — the brain's chemical associated with anticipation and reward. For developing brains, which are especially sensitive to social feedback, these cycles can become compelling quickly.

This is not dramatic addiction.

It is reinforcement.

Intermittent rewards — unpredictable responses, random likes, sporadic messages — are particularly powerful. The brain learns: "Check again. Something might be there."

For adolescents whose executive function is still strengthening, resisting that pull requires regulation that may not yet be fully developed.

Understanding this reduces blame.

You are not fighting defiance.

You are helping manage stimulation.

Look at Patterns, Not Moments

Before making changes, observe patterns.

Is the issue:

Sleep erosion?

Emotional volatility?

Academic distraction?

Compulsive checking?

Escalating conflict?

Choose the pattern that concerns you most.

Target one adjustment at a time.

Overcorrecting creates resistance.

Strategic adjustment builds cooperation.

Start With Sleep

If nothing else changes, protect sleep.

Sleep is foundational for emotional regulation and executive function. During adolescence, circadian rhythms naturally shift later. Adding blue light exposure and late-night social stimulation compounds that challenge.

Move charging stations outside the bedroom.

Establish a consistent digital cut-off time.

Explain the reason calmly:

"Sleep protects your brain."

Avoid moralizing.

Avoid dramatizing.

Sleep boundaries feel less negotiable when framed as health, not control.

Within weeks, mood often stabilizes noticeably.

Many parents are surprised how much tension decreases when sleep improves.

Shrink the Social Window

If group chat intensity feels overwhelming, reduce exposure without eliminating connection.

You might say:

"Let's limit chat checking to certain times."

"Let's step back from late-night threads."

"Let's mute some conversations."

Muting is not exclusion.

It is self-regulation.

Teach your child that stepping back is strength — not weakness.

Adolescents often assume constant availability equals loyalty.

Helping them understand that healthy limits build resilience protects them long-term.

Remove, Don't Threaten

When adjustments are needed, act without threat.

Instead of:

"If this continues, I'll take it away."

Say:

"We need to rebalance."

Then rebalance.

Children respond more predictably to calm action than escalating warnings.

Consistency builds credibility.

Threats create anxiety.

Calm structure creates stability.

Reintroduce Structure

Sometimes the issue is not the device.

It is the absence of structure around it.

Re-establish:

Phone-free meals.

Phone-free homework blocks.

Phone-free family time.

Ambient distraction erodes attention slowly and invisibly.

When notifications remain within reach — even unused — cognitive load increases.

Attention fragments.

Restoring structure restores focus.

Address Emotional Dependence

If your child appears dependent on validation — checking reactions repeatedly, feeling distressed when responses lag — acknowledge it gently.

"I notice it seems stressful when no one responds."

Invite reflection.

Curiosity lowers defensiveness.

Defensiveness blocks change.

You might ask:

"What does it feel like when no one replies right away?"

The goal is awareness, not shame.

Awareness precedes self-regulation.

When children begin naming their emotional response to digital silence, they gain distance from it.

A Temporary Reset

In some cases, a temporary reset may be necessary.

Reducing app access.

Removing social media temporarily.

Returning to basic texting for a period.

Frame it as training.

"We need to strengthen some skills."

Not punishment.

Not accusation.

Executive function grows through supported practice.

Reducing intensity while strengthening regulation allows capacity to catch up with exposure.

Children are more cooperative when they understand purpose.

Model Your Own Adjustment

If your child sees you recalibrating your own digital habits, the conversation changes.

You might say:

"I've been on my phone too much too."

Shared adjustment reduces power struggle.

Digital regulation is a family skill, not a child flaw.

When families adjust together, resistance softens.

Modeling pause, muting notifications, or leaving your phone outside the bedroom reinforces credibility.

Watch for Improvement

After recalibration, observe again.

Is sleep improving?

Is mood steadier?

Is reactivity decreasing?

Small improvements matter.

Acknowledge them.

"You seem more relaxed lately."

Change that is noticed becomes identity.

When Deeper Issues Surface

Sometimes smartphone instability reveals deeper vulnerabilities:

Anxiety.

Social insecurity.

Attention challenges.

Technology often magnifies existing struggles.

Removing the magnifier helps.

But strengthening the foundation resolves the issue more fully.

If digital conflict consistently escalates despite structure, professional guidance may help.

There is no shame in support.

Leadership includes knowing when to seek reinforcement.

Reclaiming Authority

It is common for parents to feel they have lost leverage after granting a smartphone.

Authority does not disappear with permission.

Authority shifts.

It becomes collaborative.

Calm authority sounds like:

"We need to adjust this."

Not:

"You're addicted."

"You can't handle anything."

Language determines whether the conversation builds strength or defensiveness.

The Long-Term Perspective

Even if integration began earlier than ideal, development continues.

Children grow.

Maturity increases.

Habits evolve.

The adolescent brain is adaptable.

Patterns can change.

Structure can stabilize.

Relationship can deepen.

Early introduction does not lock in permanent instability.

What matters most is not when the device arrived.

It is how you guide its use now.

The Core Reframe

The smartphone is not a verdict.
　It is an environment.
　Environments can be redesigned.
　You are not correcting a mistake.
　You are refining a process.
　Leadership is not about perfect timing.
　It is about responsive adjustment.
　If something feels off, adjust calmly.
　If something improves, reinforce it.
　Parenting is not static.
　Neither is digital integration.
　There is room to strengthen — even after yes.

13

Repairing Digital Overexposure

Sometimes the issue is not access.

It is saturation.

The device is present.

The boundaries exist.

But something still feels off.

Your child seems wired at night.

Flat during the day.

Irritable when interrupted.

Distracted even without notifications.

They are not necessarily misusing the phone.

They are simply immersed too deeply, too often.

This is overexposure.

And overexposure is not a moral failing.

It is a nervous system response.

The good news:

The nervous system is adaptable.

But it requires deliberate recalibration.

The Overstimulation Cycle

Digital platforms are engineered for stimulation.

Notifications trigger anticipation.

Scrolling triggers novelty.

Group chats trigger emotional shifts.

Social media triggers comparison.

Each stimulus produces a small dopamine release — the brain's reward chemical.

Dopamine itself is not harmful.

It drives motivation.

But frequent micro-rewards train the brain to seek stimulation more often.

When stimulation becomes constant, baseline tolerance shifts.

Silence feels dull.

Stillness feels uncomfortable.

Homework feels slower.

Conversation feels less engaging.

This is not dramatic addiction.

It is conditioning.

And conditioning can be reshaped.

Recognizing the Signs

Overexposure often appears gradually.

Your child may:

Check their phone reflexively.

Feel restless when separated from it.

Lose track of time easily.

Struggle to concentrate on slower tasks.

Appear emotionally flat or overly reactive.

The shift is subtle.

But when you step back, the contrast becomes clear.

The Reset Begins With Reduction

Repair does not require elimination.

It requires reduction.

Lowering input allows the nervous system to recalibrate.

Start with one category:

Social media.

Late-night messaging.

Endless video consumption.

Shrink the volume.

Not through punishment.

Through structure.

"Let's scale this back for a while."

Clarity reduces conflict.

Purpose reduces resistance.

Replace, Don't Just Remove

If you remove stimulation without replacement, boredom intensifies and resistance rises.

Replace digital intensity with physical engagement.

Movement.

Outdoor time.

Hands-on activities.

Sports.

Music.

Cooking.

Anything that requires focused attention without screens.

Physical engagement restores baseline dopamine sensitivity.

It stabilizes mood.

It reduces craving for constant novelty.

Protect Deep Sleep Aggressively

Sleep repair is the fastest way to reset emotional volatility.

Deep sleep regulates dopamine receptors.

It stabilizes mood.

It improves impulse control.

If your child is chronically overstimulated, prioritize sleep for several weeks.

Consistent bedtime.

No devices an hour before sleep.

Calm evening routine.

Sleep recalibrates faster than debate ever will.

Tolerate Withdrawal Discomfort

When stimulation decreases, discomfort may rise temporarily.

Irritability.

Restlessness.

Complaints of boredom.

This phase is predictable.

The brain is adjusting to lower stimulation levels.

Do not interpret this as failure.

Interpret it as recalibration.

Stay calm.

Stay consistent.

Discomfort fades as baseline shifts.

Rebuilding Boredom Tolerance

One of the most powerful long-term repairs is restoring boredom tolerance.

Encourage unstructured time.

Not as punishment.

As training.

Let your child sit without immediate input.
The first minutes may feel uncomfortable.
But creativity often emerges from emptiness.
When children rediscover internal stimulation, dependency weakens.

Restore Face-to-Face Micro-Connections

Overexposure can weaken subtle social engagement.
Encourage small in-person interactions.
Short conversations.
Shared tasks.
Eye contact.
Laughter without a device nearby.
Face-to-face connection stabilizes emotional tone.
It reminds the nervous system that belonging does not require notification.

Watch the Emotional Baseline Shift

After several weeks of reduction, you may notice:
Longer focus periods.
Less reactive mood.
More engagement in offline tasks.
Reduced urgency around checking.
These are signs of recalibration.
Reinforce gently.
"You seem more relaxed lately."
Awareness strengthens self-monitoring.
Self-monitoring strengthens regulation.

Address the Underlying Driver

Sometimes overexposure masks something deeper:

Anxiety.

Social insecurity.

Loneliness.

Boredom without direction.

If digital immersion filled an emotional gap, removing it reveals the gap.

Do not rush to refill it digitally.

Fill it relationally.

Conversation.

Shared time.

Interest development.

Emotional reassurance.

Devices often amplify unmet needs.

Meeting those needs directly reduces overexposure organically.

Gradual Reintroduction

After recalibration, reintroduce stimulation gradually.

Re-expand app access slowly.

Monitor emotional patterns.

Watch for old habits returning.

If instability resurfaces quickly, capacity may still be strengthening.

Repair is not linear.

Adjustment is normal.

No Shame, No Drama

Shame destabilizes.

Drama escalates.

Digital recalibration should feel calm.

Matter-of-fact.

"This was too much. We're adjusting."
Authority does not require intensity.
Intensity weakens authority.
Calm leadership builds trust.

The Long View of Recovery

Children adapt remarkably well when guided steadily.
Neural pathways shift with practice.
Habits weaken with reduced reinforcement.
Stimulation tolerance recalibrates.
Overexposure does not define trajectory.
It signals mismatch.
And mismatch can be corrected.
The goal is not perfect digital behavior.
It is balanced nervous system functioning.
When stimulation aligns with capacity, digital life becomes manageable.
When it exceeds capacity, strain rises.
Your role is to observe and recalibrate.
Not react and regret.
Repair is possible.

And often, it strengthens both regulation and relationship in the process.

14

Raising a Digitally Mature Teen

Eventually, this conversation is no longer about a twelve-year-old.
It is about a fifteen-year-old.
A seventeen-year-old.

A young adult who will carry a device into college, work, relationships, and independent life.

The question shifts from access to identity.

Not:

Does my child have a smartphone?

But:

Who is my child becoming inside a digital world?

Digital maturity is not about knowing how to use an app.

It is about knowing how to use yourself inside it.

Identity Before Amplification

Digital platforms amplify identity.

They do not build it.

Adolescence is a critical period of identity formation. Teens experiment with roles, values, and belonging before stabilizing into a clearer sense of self.

When this process unfolds primarily in physical communities — school, sports, friendships, family — feedback is contextual. Nuanced. Temporary.

Digital platforms intensify feedback.

Public.

Archived.

Quantified.

If your teen enters this stage without a stable sense of self, digital environments may shape identity more than reflect it.

When identity is fragile, feedback feels defining.

When identity is grounded, feedback feels informational.

A grounded teen may still care about reactions.

But they are not ruled by them.

They can post without obsessing.

Disagree without unraveling.

Step away without panic.

Identity stability determines digital resilience.

Validation vs. Self-Worth

Adolescence naturally involves validation seeking.

Teens look to peers for reflection. That is developmentally normal.

But there is a difference between healthy validation and dependency.

Healthy validation sounds like:

"That felt good."

Dependency sounds like:

"I need that again."

Digital environments make validation measurable.

Likes.

Views.

Comments.

Shares.

Metrics replace subtlety.

When self-worth becomes tied to numbers, emotional stability fluctuates.

Neuroscience shows that adolescent brains are especially sensitive to social reward signals. The same neural regions that respond to peer approval respond to digital metrics.

This makes checking behavior especially compelling during teenage years.

The digitally mature teen understands something critical:

Metrics measure attention — not value.

That understanding protects emotional equilibrium.

The Capacity to Step Away

One of the clearest indicators of digital maturity is the ability to disengage.

Can your teen:

Mute a conversation?

Ignore a provocation?

Close an app voluntarily?

Delay a response?

Impulse control in digital spaces mirrors impulse control offline.

Executive function — planning, inhibition, emotional control — continues strengthening throughout adolescence.

If stepping away feels intolerable, maturity is still forming.

If stepping away feels neutral — even relieving — regulation is strengthening.

The ability to disconnect is not weakness.

It is sovereignty.

Navigating Public Mistakes

Teens will make mistakes.

A poorly judged comment.

A joke that lands wrong.

A photo they regret.

A message sent too quickly.

The question is not whether mistakes happen.

It is how they are integrated.

Digitally mature teens:

Acknowledge missteps.

Repair when necessary.

Learn without collapsing.

They do not catastrophize.

They do not double down defensively.

Repair is maturity in action.

Without repair, digital history compounds.

With repair, growth becomes visible.

Parents can model this. When you misstep online, acknowledge it. Apologize without drama. Show that accountability strengthens credibility.

Teens absorb that lesson deeply.

Managing Comparison Without Collapse

Comparison intensifies during adolescence.

Bodies change.

Social groups shift.

Romantic dynamics emerge.

Digital platforms amplify visibility of all of it.

The mature teen recognizes curated reality.

They understand that posts represent highlights — not whole lives.

They may feel comparison.

But they contextualize it.

They do not internalize every image as judgment.

This skill does not develop automatically.

It must be discussed.

Without conversation, comparison becomes silent and corrosive.

With conversation, comparison becomes navigable.

Ask:

"What do you think that photo doesn't show?"

Questions expand perspective.

Perspective reduces distortion.

The Courage to Be Unimpressed

Digital culture rewards trend alignment.
Being early.
Being viral.
Being visible.
A digitally mature teen can be unimpressed.
They can decline participation in trends that feel misaligned.
Resist pressure to share everything.
Remain quiet when others escalate.
This quiet confidence often comes from identity anchored offline.
When identity has roots beyond digital spaces — athletics, art, academics, community — digital waves feel less destabilizing.
Diversified identity stabilizes mood.

Emotional Regulation in Public

Adolescence includes emotional intensity.
Breakups.
Friendship shifts.
Academic stress.
Digital platforms tempt public processing.
The mature teen learns discernment.
Not every emotion needs an audience.
Not every thought needs broadcasting.
Private processing builds depth.
Public processing creates exposure.
The ability to differentiate between the two marks emotional growth.

Time as a Resource

Digital maturity includes time awareness.

Teens who can estimate how long they are spending, who can pause before scrolling, who can prioritize responsibilities before engagement, demonstrate strengthening executive function.

Time blindness is common in adolescence.

But with guidance, awareness grows.

The goal is not rigid control.

It is conscious choice.

A mature teen may still scroll.

But they know when to stop.

The Role of Ongoing Conversation

Digital maturity does not arrive automatically.

It develops through reflection.

Ask questions without interrogation:

"How did that feel?"

"Did you want to respond differently?"

"Was that stressful?"

Curiosity builds awareness.

Awareness builds regulation.

Regulation builds independence.

Silence allows confusion to compound.

Conversation stabilizes.

Technology as Tool, Not Identity

When digital identity becomes primary identity, instability increases.

A teen who defines themselves by platform engagement risks emotional volatility when engagement fluctuates.

Encourage diversified identity:

Athletics.
Creative work.
Academic interests.
Community involvement.
Real-world skill building.
When identity spans multiple domains, digital shifts feel smaller.
Smaller shifts produce steadier moods.

Preparing for Full Autonomy

The ultimate goal is not compliance under your roof.
It is discernment beyond it.
When your teen leaves home, you will not control their device.
You will not monitor their usage.
You will not manage their boundaries.
What you can build is internal regulation.
Internal regulation persists without supervision.
Surveillance does not.
Gradual autonomy teaches self-management.
Overcontrol delays it.
You are not raising a rule-follower.
You are raising a self-governor.

Modeling Digital Maturity

Teens watch adults closely.
If you respond impulsively to online conflict,
If you scroll reflexively,
If you react emotionally to digital content,
They absorb that.
Modeling calm digital behavior teaches more effectively than lectures.
Pause before reacting.
Close apps intentionally.

Protect your own sleep.
Maturity replicates.

The Core Shift

Digital maturity is not about eliminating mistakes.
It is about integrating them.
It is not about avoiding comparison.
It is about contextualizing it.
It is not about disengaging entirely.
It is about engaging deliberately.
The device is not the developmental challenge.
Identity is.
If identity strengthens first, digital life integrates more smoothly.
If digital immersion precedes identity formation, instability increases.
Your long-term aim is not to control access.
It is to build character strong enough to navigate access.
When character leads, technology follows.

That is digital maturity.

15

Building a Family Digital Culture

Every family already has a digital culture.

Some families simply haven't named it.

It appears in small moments:

Phones at dinner.

Notifications during conversation.

Screens in bedrooms.

Scrolling during commercials.

Checking messages mid-sentence.

Children do not only absorb rules.

They absorb rhythm.

And rhythm shapes regulation.

Behavioral science consistently shows that environment influences habit formation more than intention alone. Repeated exposure to cues — a buzzing phone, a glowing screen, a reflexive reach — creates automatic patterns.

If digital life feels frantic in the home, children internalize urgency.

If digital life feels contained, children internalize steadiness.

Before focusing on your child's habits, examine the household pattern.

Because regulation spreads.

And so does dysregulation.

A Small Mirror Moment

A father once described asking his son to stop checking his phone during homework.

His son responded calmly:

"You check yours during dinner."

The room went quiet.

The father was not careless.

He was automatic.

That moment revealed something powerful:

Children mirror what feels normal.

Not what feels instructed.

Digital culture is transmitted far more through modeling than through rules.

The Tone You Set

Children measure digital importance by adult reaction.

If every notification pulls your attention instantly, it signals hierarchy.

The device outranks the room.

If you pause before checking, it signals choice.

Choice models agency.

Psychologists call this social learning — children internalize what they observe repeatedly.

You do not need perfection.

You need intention.

Subtle shifts communicate power:

Putting the phone face down during conversation.

Leaving it in another room during meals.

Finishing a thought before responding to a buzz.

These moments teach without speeches.

Shared Boundaries Feel Fair

Rules applied only to children create resistance.

Boundaries shared across the household create credibility.

If you expect devices out of bedrooms at night, consider doing the same.

If you want tech-free family time, participate fully.

Fairness builds trust.

Trust strengthens authority.

Authority without hypocrisy builds respect.

Alignment reduces cognitive dissonance — the discomfort children feel when expectations and modeling conflict.

Consistency builds stability.

Meals as Anchors

Family meals are one of the simplest digital resets.

No devices at the table.

Conversation uninterrupted.

Eye contact unbroken.

It may feel uncomfortable at first.

Silence may stretch.

That discomfort reveals how accustomed we are to constant stimulation.

Protecting shared meals protects relational rhythm.

Relational rhythm stabilizes emotional tone.

Emotional tone influences digital regulation.

Research consistently links shared family meals with improved emotional well-being and communication in adolescents. The benefit is not the food — it is undistracted presence.

Presence builds security.

Designated Tech Zones

Physical boundaries simplify discipline.

Charging stations in common areas.

No devices upstairs after a certain hour.

Clear places for usage.

Habit research shows behavior changes more easily when environmental cues shift.

Moving devices out of bedrooms reduces temptation without constant willpower.

Structure makes discipline less personal.

It becomes environmental rather than emotional.

Children adapt to environmental design faster than repeated lectures.

Modeling Disconnection

One of the most powerful lessons you can teach is deliberate disconnection.

Say it aloud.

"I'm putting my phone away for an hour."

"I don't need to check that right now."

When disconnection becomes visible, it becomes normalized.

Children learn that constant access is optional.

Optional access builds self-control.

Compulsive access erodes it.

Self-regulation strengthens through repetition.

Every intentional pause reinforces restraint.

Technology-Free Rituals

Establish rituals untouched by screens.

Weekly walks.

Game nights.

Reading time.

Shared cooking.

Religious or spiritual practice.

Rituals create stability.

Stability buffers digital intensity.

When certain spaces are reliably device-free, the nervous system relaxes.

Predictable structure lowers background stress.

Those calm pockets matter more than they seem.

Open Dialogue Without Surveillance

A strong digital culture includes conversation — not interrogation.

Ask:

"What's trending lately?"

"Anything stressful online?"

"How do people handle conflict in chats?"

Curiosity signals interest, not suspicion.

If children feel monitored constantly, secrecy increases.

If they feel safe discussing digital life, insight increases.

Insight builds regulation.

Reflection strengthens executive function.

Normalize Mixed Feelings

Digital life is not entirely harmful.

It brings humor.

Connection.

Information.

Creativity.

A healthy culture acknowledges both benefit and strain.

Avoid extremes.

"Phones ruin everything."

Or:

"It's just how life is now."

Both oversimplify.
Nuance builds trust.
Trust fosters openness.
Openness protects children better than fear.

Protect Sleep Collectively

If sleep rules apply only to children, inconsistency undermines authority.
A family-wide digital wind-down strengthens discipline.
Dimming lights.
Reducing notifications.
Shifting to quieter activities.
Sleep science consistently shows that screen exposure before bed can delay melatonin release and disrupt cycles.
Sleep protects emotional regulation.
Without reset, volatility increases.
Protecting sleep is not restriction.
It is brain protection.

Repair When Culture Slips

Even strong digital cultures drift.
Busy weeks.
Travel.
Stress.
Habits loosen.
When you notice drift, recalibrate calmly.
"We've been on devices more lately."
"Let's reset this week."
No blame.
No drama.
Just course correction.
Consistency matters more than perfection.

Children learn resilience when they see recovery modeled.

Teach Digital Discernment

Digital maturity includes content awareness.
Not everything deserves attention.
Not every message deserves response.
Teach your child to ask:
Is this worth my energy?
Is this helpful?
Is this aligned with who I am?
Discernment protects identity.
Identity protects emotional stability.
Without discernment, digital life dictates mood.
With discernment, your child directs it.

The Energy in the Room

Observe your household during quiet moments.
Is there calm?
Or restless scrolling?
Do conversations linger?
Or end abruptly when notifications interrupt?
Energy is contagious.
Fragmented attention reduces emotional depth.
Depth builds resilience.
Protect depth.

The Goal of Family Digital Culture

You are not eliminating technology.
You are containing it.
Containment prevents spillover.

Spillover erodes boundaries.

Boundaries create psychological safety.

Psychological safety builds trust.

Trust strengthens communication.

Communication protects your child far more than restriction alone.

The Long View

Your child will eventually leave your home.

What remains will not be your Wi-Fi password.

It will be your modeling.

Your tone.

Your rhythms.

Your norms.

If your home demonstrates balanced digital engagement, your child carries that template forward.

Family culture is invisible but powerful.

It shapes instinct.

Instinct guides behavior when no one is watching.

And digital life is often unwatched.

Build a culture that supports regulation.

Devices will evolve.

Culture remains.

16

What Schools Aren't Teaching About Digital Life

Schools teach algebra.

They teach grammar.

They teach history, biology, and the structure of atoms.

They teach essays, equations, and exam preparation.

What they rarely teach — at least not explicitly — is how to live inside a digital world without being consumed by it.

And yet, that may be one of the most essential skills your child will need.

Not how to code.

Not how to use software.

But how to manage attention.

How to regulate emotion under constant stimulation.

How to interpret tone without facial cues.

How to disengage from conflict without escalation.

These are not minor skills.

They are foundational.

Attention Is Now a Battleground

Your child's attention is valuable.

Not metaphorically.

Economically.

Digital platforms are engineered to capture and hold it.

Notifications.

Autoplay.

Infinite scroll.

Algorithmic content selection.

Each feature extends engagement.

This is not conspiracy.

It is business design.

Adults struggle in this environment.

Children — whose executive function is still developing — are especially vulnerable to distraction.

Schools expect sustained focus.

Digital platforms reward fragmentation.

That tension is rarely addressed directly.

Executive Function Is Still Developing

Executive function includes:

Impulse control.

Planning.

Time management.

Working memory.

Emotional regulation.

These capacities strengthen gradually through adolescence.

Yet digital environments demand high executive function immediately.

Ignore notifications.

Resist endless scroll.

Manage time independently.

Interpret ambiguous tone.

Children are asked to perform advanced regulation inside systems designed to undermine it.

Without explicit training, many default to impulse.

Impulse is not immaturity.

It is developmental reality meeting engineered stimulation.

Emotional Literacy in a Text-Only World

Digital communication removes nonverbal cues.

No eye contact.

No tone inflection.

No immediate facial feedback.

Children must interpret meaning through text alone.

Sarcasm can appear harsh.

Humor can look cruel.

Silence can look intentional.

Without emotional literacy — the ability to identify and regulate internal states — misinterpretation increases.

Schools teach writing mechanics.

They rarely teach tone interpretation under emotional pressure.

Parents must fill that gap.

Conflict Moves Faster Online

Conflict once unfolded in contained spaces.

Now it follows children home.

A disagreement at lunch can continue into the evening.

Screenshots spread.

Private messages circulate.

Rumors amplify.

Speed compresses reaction time.

Children must decide quickly:

Respond?

Ignore?

Escalate?

Retreat?

Without training, reaction becomes instinct.

Instinct under stress is rarely measured.

Measured response requires practice.

The Skill of Pause

One of the most powerful digital skills is pause.

Pause before posting.

Pause before responding.

Pause before reacting.

Pause before forwarding.

But pause is countercultural online.

Speed signals relevance.

Delayed response feels risky.

Teach pause explicitly.

"You don't have to answer right away."

"Draft it. Don't send it yet."

"Take a minute before replying."

Pause protects reputation.

It protects relationships.

It protects identity.

Attention Literacy

Children are rarely taught to examine how platforms shape what they see.

Ask:

Why do you think this video appeared?

Why did that post go viral?

What kinds of content seem to spread fastest?

When children understand that algorithms prioritize emotionally charged material, they gain perspective.

They see that outrage spreads faster than nuance.

Conflict spreads faster than cooperation.

Perspective reduces internalization.

Internalization increases volatility.

Managing Digital Reputation

Before social media, adolescence allowed reinvention.

Mistakes faded.

Embarrassing phases passed.

Now digital records persist.

Schools may mention digital footprint in passing.

Parents must deepen the conversation.

Discuss permanence.

Discuss screenshots.

Discuss how tone may be misread years later.

Not to instill fear.

To build foresight.

Foresight is executive function in action.

Teaching Emotional Boundaries

Children must learn:

Not every opinion requires response.

Not every comment requires defense.

Not every provocation deserves energy.

Digital maturity includes selective engagement.

Selective engagement protects emotional reserves.

Without it, attention becomes reactive.

Reactive attention increases stress.

Schools teach academic resilience.

Parents must cultivate digital resilience.

The Cost of Multitasking

Many students attempt homework while messaging.
Research consistently shows multitasking reduces cognitive efficiency.
Switching between tasks increases mental fatigue.
Fatigue lowers impulse control.
Lower impulse control increases digital overuse.
It becomes a loop.
Teaching focused work blocks — devices out of reach — strengthens executive function.
Executive function stabilizes digital life.

Social Courage Offline

Schools teach collaboration.
They do not always teach face-to-face repair.
Encourage your child to practice uncomfortable conversations offline.
Asking for clarification.
Addressing misunderstandings directly.
Apologizing in person.
These skills transfer powerfully into digital life.
Without them, avoidance becomes default.
Avoidance compounds anxiety.

Curating Influence

Children consume enormous volumes of content.
Few are taught to curate it intentionally.
Ask:
Does this content leave you energized or drained?
Inspired or insecure?

Calm or agitated?
Teaching reflective consumption builds agency.
Agency reduces passive comparison.
Passive comparison erodes self-worth.

The Missing Curriculum

If schools do not formally teach digital regulation, responsibility shifts to the home.
Not through lectures.
Through modeling.
Through conversation.
Through steady boundaries.
Through calm recalibration.
Digital literacy is not simply operating technology.
It is operating yourself within it.

The Long View

Your child will graduate.
Digital fluency will be assumed.
But digital fluency without self-regulation is fragile.
Self-regulation without digital fluency is incomplete.
The goal is integration.
Strong executive function.
Clear emotional literacy.
Stable identity.
Conscious attention.
These skills are rarely graded.
But they determine long-term stability far more than test scores in a digital age.
Schools may teach information.
You teach discernment.

Discernment protects your child inside complexity.

And complexity is not decreasing.

17

When Other Parents Disagree

At some point, the pressure shifts.

It is no longer your child arguing.

It is other adults.

"Most kids have one by now."

"It's safer if they can text."

"You don't want them to be the only one."

Sometimes it is subtle.

A raised eyebrow.

A surprised tone.

A quick comparison.

Other times it is direct.

"You're being too strict."

"You're overthinking it."

"You'll regret waiting."

These conversations can feel destabilizing.

Not because the arguments are strong.

But because no parent wants to feel unreasonable.

Adult Comparison Is Real

Parents compare timelines the way children compare devices.

Who introduced earlier.

Who delayed longer.

Who seems relaxed.

Who seems rigid.

It is easy to absorb another parent's confidence as proof that you are uncertain.

But parenting decisions are not transferable templates.

What works in one home may not align in another.

Temperament differs.

Family culture differs.

Capacity differs.

Your responsibility is not to match consensus.

It is to match development.

When Safety Becomes Leverage

One of the most persuasive arguments from other parents involves safety.

"They need one for emergencies."

"It's safer if you can track them."

Safety concerns are valid.

But safety tools do not require full digital immersion.

A basic phone provides emergency access.

Location sharing can exist without social media.

Separate emergency utility from social platform exposure.

Safety should not become shorthand for unlimited access.

Clarity prevents conflation.

The Fear of Social Isolation

Other parents often express concern on your behalf.
"You don't want them left out."
The implication is that delay equals disadvantage.
But inclusion is more complex than ownership.
You can gently ask:
"Have you actually seen kids lose friendships over this?"
Often the answer is anecdotal.
Fear spreads quickly in parenting communities.
Fear feels protective.
But fear is not always predictive.

Confidence Without Superiority

Tone determines whether disagreement escalates or dissolves.
Avoid moral framing.
Avoid suggesting your approach is more enlightened.
You can simply say:
"We're waiting a bit."
"This timing works for us."
"We're building skills first."
Confidence without superiority reduces defensiveness.
Defensiveness escalates conflict.
Calm neutrality diffuses it.

Hidden Anxiety Among Adults

Strong opinions sometimes mask private uncertainty.
Another parent may feel uneasy about their own timing.
They may worry about overexposure.
They may fear being judged as too permissive.
Your steadiness can surface their discomfort.

You do not need to absorb it.
Let it remain theirs.

When Your Child Compares Families

Your child may say:
"Other parents don't care."
"They trust their kids."
"They're not strict."
This is less about policy and more about perception.
Children often interpret boundaries as mistrust.
Reframe calmly:
"Trust grows with responsibility."
"We're building toward that."
"This isn't about control. It's about timing."
Boundaries without explanation feel arbitrary.
Boundaries with explanation feel purposeful.

Avoid the Defensive Spiral

It is tempting to justify extensively.
To cite research.
To debate developmental timelines.
To defend your reasoning in detail.
You do not owe a thesis.
Overexplaining can signal insecurity.
Short, clear alignment works better:
"This feels right for our family right now."
Simple statements carry strength.

The Value of Aligned Community

If possible, find even one family with similar timing.
  Children feel less isolated when peers share boundaries.
  Parents feel steadier when not alone.
  Alignment reduces social friction.
  But alignment is not required.
  Leadership sometimes means standing slightly apart.

Modeling Respect for Other Choices

Speak neutrally about other families' decisions.
  Avoid criticism.
  Children listen closely.
  If you speak harshly about permissive parents, your child may internalize superiority.
  Superiority strains peer relationships.
  Neutrality preserves them.

Patience Over Popularity

Parenting culture moves quickly.
  Trends shift.
  New apps emerge.
  Consensus evolves.
  A decision that feels unconventional this year may feel standard next year.
  You are making a developmental choice.
  Not a popularity choice.
  Patience protects perspective.

When Doubt Creeps In

There will be moments when you question yourself.

After a social event.

After a difficult conversation.

After hearing another parent speak confidently.

Doubt is normal.

Pause before reacting to it.

Return to your criteria.

Is your child building capacity?

Is their emotional baseline stable?

Are friendships intact?

Is your relationship strong?

Clarity quiets doubt.

The Long-Term Metric

Years from now, you will not measure success by whether you matched other parents' timelines.

You will measure:

Your child's stability.

Their confidence.

Their ability to regulate emotion independently.

Their relationship with you.

These metrics unfold slowly.

Short-term comparison obscures long-term trajectory.

Leading Quietly

Strong parenting often looks unremarkable from the outside.

It does not trend.

It does not win debates.

It unfolds gradually.

You do not need consensus.
You need alignment with your child's development.
Other parents' opinions will fluctuate.
Your child's trajectory is what remains.
Lead calmly.
Disagree quietly.
Stay steady.
Steadiness transfers.

And children borrow steadiness from adults who carry it well.

18

When You're the Only Family Delaying

There may come a moment when it feels like you are the last one.

The last parent waiting.

The last household without a group chat.

The last birthday without a smartphone gift.

It can feel isolating — not just for your child, but for you.

The conversation shifts from developmental timing to social courage.

Because standing apart is uncomfortable.

Especially when what you are resisting looks normal everywhere else.

The Illusion of Universality

When something becomes common, it feels inevitable.

If most of your child's friends have smartphones, the absence in your home feels conspicuous.

But common does not equal correct.

Common does not equal optimal.

Cultural shifts move quickly.

Development moves gradually.

Technology adoption spreads rapidly.

Maturity strengthens slowly.

Speed of adoption does not guarantee readiness.

It guarantees normalization.

The Quiet Strength of Conviction

When you are the only one delaying, the temptation is to soften your stance.
To apologize for it.
To frame it as temporary weakness.
Resist that impulse.
You do not need to defend your timing as superior.
But you also do not need to present it as deficiency.
Confidence is quiet.
"We're waiting a bit."
No elaboration required.
Children sense whether you believe your own decision.
If you waver publicly, they internalize uncertainty.
If you stand calmly, they borrow your steadiness.

Preparing Your Child for Being Different

Your child may say:
"I'm the only one."
That feeling deserves validation.
It may be true in their immediate circle.
Being slightly different socially is a developmental challenge.
But challenge is not harm.
Equip your child with simple language:
"My parents are waiting."
"It's coming later."
"We're doing it differently."
Neutral. Calm. Brief.
Lengthy explanations invite debate.
Short statements signal security.

Differentiation as a Skill

Learning to tolerate being slightly outside the norm builds differentiation.

Differentiation is the ability to maintain identity without dissolving into group pressure.

It is one of the most protective long-term traits.

Teens who can say no without losing themselves navigate risk more effectively.

Delaying a smartphone can become early practice in differentiation.

Not isolation.

Identity.

Watch for Real Isolation

Standing apart socially can build strength.

But monitor carefully.

If your child begins withdrawing...

If invitations decrease sharply...

If mood declines persistently...

Reassess.

Standing apart should build confidence, not erode it.

Mild discomfort strengthens.

Chronic distress signals misalignment.

Discernment matters.

The Cultural Echo Chamber

Your immediate social circle may amplify pressure.

If most families nearby adopt early, it can feel universal.

Remember: your community sample is small.

Adoption rates vary widely by region, culture, and temperament.

Perspective reduces urgency.

Your household may feel like an outlier locally.

It is not an outlier globally.

Modeling Comfort With Difference

Children learn how to hold difference by watching adults hold difference.
If you speak resentfully about other families, your child absorbs tension.
If you speak calmly and neutrally, your child absorbs confidence.
Difference handled with grace becomes strength.
Difference handled with hostility becomes burden.
Your tone determines which.

Reframing "Behind"

Children often equate later access with being behind.
Reframe gently:
"You're not behind. You're preparing."
Behind suggests deficiency.
Preparing suggests intention.
Language shapes identity.
Identity shapes resilience.
Resilience reduces insecurity.

The Advantage of Deliberate Timing

There is quiet power in entering a space slightly later.
Novelty has worn off.
Peer mistakes have surfaced.
You have observed patterns.
When your child eventually joins, they do so with awareness.
Awareness protects stability.
Rushing rarely improves outcomes.
Observation often does.

The Emotional Work of Standing Alone

Parents may feel isolated too.
Other adults may question your decision.
You may question it privately.
It takes courage to hold a boundary when culture pushes forward.
Return to your criteria:
Capacity.
Regulation.
Identity strength.
If those remain central, pressure loses urgency.

A Temporary Phase

Very few children remain the only one forever.
Circles expand.
Peer groups shift.
More families reconsider timing.
Temporary difference does not define long-term status.
Perspective protects peace.

The Core Question

When you feel alone in delay, return to one question:
Am I acting from fear — or from clarity?
If fear drives delay, reconsider.
If clarity drives delay, remain steady.
Clarity withstands pressure.
Fear reacts to it.
Your child benefits more from clear leadership than from social conformity.

The Long View of Courage

Standing slightly apart builds courage.
  Courage strengthens identity.
  Identity stabilizes digital engagement later.
  You are not isolating your child by default.
  You are pacing development intentionally.
  Sometimes that pace differs from the crowd.
  Crowds move quickly.
  Maturity moves steadily.
  Steady often outlasts fast.
  Hold your timing with calm conviction.

Your child is learning how to stand by watching you stand first.

19

When to Reevaluate

No parenting decision should become permanent simply because it was once correct.

Children change.

Circumstances change.

Maturity grows.

Pressure shifts.

What felt aligned at eleven may feel misaligned at thirteen.

Reevaluation is not surrender.

It is responsiveness.

And responsiveness is strength.

The Difference Between Panic and Reflection

Reevaluation should not happen in reaction to a single uncomfortable moment.

A missed party.

A difficult conversation.

A comparison with another family.

Panic-driven decisions create instability.

Reflection-driven decisions build trust.

Pause before adjusting.

Look for patterns, not spikes.

Patterns reveal trajectory.

Spikes reflect emotion.

Signals That Growth Has Occurred

There may come a time when you notice subtle shifts.

Your child recovers from disappointment faster.

Handles conflict with less intensity.

Accepts boundaries without prolonged resistance.

Manages responsibilities more consistently.

Emotional volatility decreases.

Confidence increases.

These signals may not be dramatic.

They often arrive gradually.

But when capacity strengthens, alignment changes.

And alignment invites reconsideration.

External Changes Matter Too

Sometimes reevaluation is prompted by the environment, not just the child.

A transition to middle school.

Increased independence.

New extracurricular demands.

More complex scheduling.

Greater travel without parents.

Technology can support responsibility.

And responsibility may require access.

Context matters.

Timing should respond to developmental stage — not stubborn adherence to an earlier season.

Listen to the Tone of the Request

When your child revisits the conversation, listen carefully.
Does the request sound desperate — or grounded?
Entitled — or measured?
Emotionally charged — or calmly reasoned?
Tone reveals readiness.
A calmer request often signals internal growth.
Urgent pressure often signals insecurity.
Respond to tone, not volume.

Avoid Ego-Based Delay

Sometimes delay continues because of parental pride.
"I've held this long. I don't want to give in."
That framing shifts the focus from development to ego.
Reevaluation requires humility.
The goal is not to win consistency points.
The goal is to stay aligned with maturity.
If capacity has grown, acknowledge it.
Children respect leaders who adapt thoughtfully.

Watch for Real Social Impact

If your child consistently experiences isolation — not friction — reevaluation may be necessary.

Isolation includes:

Persistent exclusion
Visible social withdrawal
Mood decline tied directly to digital absence
These are not minor inconveniences.

They signal misalignment.

Adjustment may protect emotional well-being.

Protect the Core Principles

Reevaluation does not mean abandoning structure.

Even if timing shifts, core values remain:

Sleep protection.

Clear boundaries.

Gradual autonomy.

Open conversation.

Flexibility in timing does not require flexibility in principle.

Make Reevaluation an Ongoing Dialogue

Reevaluation should feel collaborative, not reactive.

You might say:

"We've noticed growth."

"Let's talk about what's changed."

"What feels different now?"

This invites reflection.

Reflection builds awareness.

Awareness builds self-regulation.

Self-regulation strengthens digital integration.

Change Does Not Equal Weakness

Some parents fear that adjusting timing will signal inconsistency.

Children do not interpret thoughtful change as weakness.

They interpret it as responsiveness.

Responsiveness builds trust.

Trust deepens communication.

Communication protects relationship.

Rigid inflexibility can erode connection.

Measured flexibility strengthens it.

The Developmental Timeline Is Long

Adolescence spans years.

Growth does not happen in one leap.

It happens in stages.

Reevaluation allows pacing to match growth.

You are not locking your child into a permanent category.

You are calibrating complexity to capacity repeatedly.

Calibration is leadership.

The Final Question

Before adjusting your timing, ask:

Has my child's capacity grown — or has my discomfort increased?

If capacity has grown, reconsider confidently.

If discomfort has increased due to pressure, pause.

Decisions rooted in clarity feel stable.

Decisions rooted in anxiety feel rushed.

Stability protects relationship.

The Balance of Courage and Flexibility

It takes courage to delay when culture accelerates.

It also takes courage to adjust when growth emerges.

Both require discernment.

Discernment requires observation.

Observation requires patience.

Your role is not to freeze a decision in time.

It is to guide development responsibly.

Reevaluation, done thoughtfully, strengthens authority rather than weakens it.

Because authority grounded in awareness remains steady — even as circumstances evolve.

20

The Long View

Years from now, you will not remember the exact day your child received a smartphone.

You may not remember the argument.

Or the hesitation.

Or the peer comparisons.

What you will remember is who they became.

Were they steady?

Self-aware?

Able to sit in discomfort without unraveling?

Able to step away when something felt wrong?

Able to navigate digital life without being consumed by it?

That is the long view.

And the long view matters more than the timeline.

Technology Will Keep Changing

The apps your child wants today will be replaced.

Platforms will rise and fall.

Group chats will migrate.

Features will evolve.

The digital landscape will not stabilize.

It will accelerate.

If your parenting strategy depends on mastering every new platform, exhaustion will follow.

But if your strategy centers on character, the environment matters less.

Character travels.

Platforms change.

You Are Raising a Nervous System

Before you are raising a device user, you are raising a nervous system.

A mind that will encounter stimulation.

A body that will experience stress.

An identity that will be reflected and reshaped by peers.

If that nervous system learns to regulate before immersion intensifies, it adapts more smoothly.

If stimulation arrives before regulation strengthens, instability increases.

Your role is not to eliminate stimulation.

It is to strengthen regulation.

Regulation outlasts trends.

Belonging Is Deeper Than Access

Your child's deepest need is not digital presence.

It is belonging.

Belonging built on:

Shared experience.

Mutual respect.

Authenticity.

Emotional safety.

Access can facilitate belonging.

But access alone cannot create it.

Belonging rooted in identity survives fluctuation.

Belonging rooted in constant validation fractures under pressure.

You are not deciding whether your child belongs.
You are shaping how they understand belonging.

Resilience Grows Quietly

Resilience does not announce itself.
It grows in small moments:
Missing a joke and recovering.
Being slightly different and staying grounded.
Asking directly instead of withdrawing.
Stepping away from conflict instead of escalating.
These micro-decisions compound.
Over years, they shape confidence.
Confidence stabilizes digital life.

Authority Evolves

As your child grows, your authority will shift.
From control to consultation.
From enforcement to guidance.
From boundaries to discernment.
The foundation you build during early conversations influences later trust.
If your child experiences you as steady — not reactive — they return to you when complexity increases.
If they experience you as anxious or rigid, distance grows.
The tone you carry matters more than the exact timing you choose.

Imperfection Is Expected

There will be mistakes.
Late nights.
Overexposure.
Misjudged posts.

Moments of regret.

Digital life guarantees imperfection.

Perfection is not the goal.

Recovery is.

If your child can apologize sincerely, adjust behavior, and regain equilibrium, they are equipped.

Equipped children navigate imperfect environments well.

Your Relationship Is the Anchor

Devices enter and exit your child's hands.

Your relationship remains.

If digital life begins to strain that relationship, recalibrate.

Connection precedes correction.

Conversation precedes enforcement.

Influence depends on trust.

Trust depends on safety.

Safety grows when your child feels heard — not managed.

The Courage to Be Measured

The culture of acceleration suggests:

Earlier is better.

Faster is better.

More connected is better.

Development does not follow cultural speed.

It follows neurological growth.

Measured timing is not backward.

It is strategic.

You are not resisting the future.

You are pacing it.

And pacing protects.

When They Leave Home

There will come a day when you cannot set limits.
When you cannot monitor.
When you cannot intervene.
On that day, what remains is internal.
Impulse control.
Emotional regulation.
Identity stability.
Discernment.
If those qualities are strong, digital life becomes manageable.
If they are fragile, digital life feels overwhelming.
Your early decisions ripple forward.
Not because of the device.
Because of the skills you strengthened first.

The Real Question

This has never been about smartphones.
It has been about formation.
Are you forming a child who can:
Pause before reacting?
Tolerate discomfort?
Recover from embarrassment?
Resist peer pressure?
Protect sleep?
Guard attention?
These qualities matter far beyond screens.
They matter in friendships.
In relationships.
In work.
In leadership.
In self-respect.

— CONFIDENCE VS. SCREEN DEPENDENCE —

Path A: Early Unrestricted Access	VS.	Path B: Structured Digital Readiness
Exposure to adult content at a young age		Safer, age-appropriate content exposure
Less motivation for real-world exploration		Emphasis on hobbies, activities, and study habits
Higher risk of digital addiction		Balanced digital habits with interests offline
Low self-esteem reliant on likes & followers		Higher confidence & independence in teens

Path A:
Early Unrestricted Access

Path B:
Structured Digital Readiness

Path A:
Early Unrestricted Access

Path B:
Structured Digital Readiness

The Quiet Confidence

You may never receive applause for pacing intentionally.
   Or for recalibrating thoughtfully.
   But quiet leadership produces quiet strength.
   And quiet strength endures.
   The device will change.
   The platforms will change.
   The pressure will change.
   But a steady nervous system.
   A grounded identity.
   A confident young adult.
   Those endure.
   That is the long view.

And the long view is worth holding.

Epilogue

The Day You Won't Notice

There will not be a dramatic moment.

No headline.

No milestone announcement.

No visible turning point where you suddenly know you handled this perfectly.

One day, your child will walk into a room, place their phone down without being told, and begin talking to you.

You may not even register it.

Another day, they will receive a message that stings — and instead of spiraling, they will pause, breathe, and move on.

You may not register that either.

One evening, they will say, "I'm going to bed," and plug their phone in outside their room.

No argument.

No reminder.

Just choice.

And it will feel ordinary.

That is the day you won't notice.

Because growth rarely announces itself.

It integrates quietly.

You may spend years wondering if you are too strict.

Too cautious.

Too reflective.

Too different from the families around you.

You may question your timing.

Your firmness.

Your flexibility.

You may wonder whether you are creating friction where ease would be simpler.

But what you are building is not ease.

You are building internal strength.

And internal strength rarely feels dramatic.

It feels like repetition.

Like steady boundaries.

Like conversations that seem small.

Like decisions no one applauds.

But repetition becomes identity.

And identity determines how a child carries themselves when no one is watching.

Technology will continue evolving.

Faster than you can track.

Louder than you prefer.

More immersive than you expect.

But your child's nervous system — their ability to regulate emotion, tolerate discomfort, and step away when needed — will matter more than the sophistication of any device.

If they can pause before reacting, they are ahead.

If they can tolerate being slightly different, they are strong.

If they can put the phone down voluntarily, they are free.

Freedom is not the absence of technology.

It is the presence of self-control.

One day, your child will enter a world fully saturated with digital noise.

They will encounter comparison.

Provocation.

Endless stimulation.

And you will not be beside them to monitor it.

What will remain is not the exact age they received a smartphone.

What will remain is the tone you carried.

The steadiness you modeled.

The boundaries you explained calmly.

The recalibrations you made without shame.

The respect you showed for their growing maturity.

That tone becomes their inner voice.

That steadiness becomes their reference point.

That respect becomes their self-respect.

There will be missteps.

Late nights.

Overexposure.

Moments of regret.

Moments when you wish you had timed something differently.

Parenting in a digital age does not offer perfection.

It offers direction.

What matters is not whether you eliminated every mistake.

It is whether your child learned to recover from them.

Recovery becomes resilience.

Resilience becomes independence.

Independence becomes discernment.

And discernment becomes freedom.

Eventually, the debates will fade.

The conversations about readiness.

The group chat tension.

The comparisons with other families.

They will recede into memory.

In their place, you will see a young adult who can sit at a table without reaching reflexively for a screen.

Who can engage in conversation without splitting attention.

Who can leave an online conflict without escalating it.

Who can walk away from a trend that does not align with who they are.

Who can exist online without being consumed by it.

That was always the goal.

Even when it felt invisible.

You were never simply raising a child without a smartphone.

You were raising a child with self-possession.

And self-possession outlasts every platform.

It outlasts every update.

It outlasts every cultural shift.

Devices will become faster.

Louder.

More immersive.

But a grounded human being remains grounded.

That is the work.

And it is worth it.

The goal was never the phone. It was who they become while holding it.

How to Read This Book

This book is not anti-technology.

It is not an argument for permanent restriction.

It is not a rigid rulebook.

And it is not a judgment on families who chose differently.

It is an invitation to pause.

In a culture that accelerates childhood, this book asks a simple question:

What does readiness actually look like?

You do not need to read this book in one sitting.

You do not need to agree with every page.

You can move slowly.

Reflect.

Pause.

Return later.

Some chapters may feel relevant right now.

Others may feel more relevant a year from now.

Childhood unfolds in stages.

This book is designed to unfold with it.

You may return to the early chapters when your child first says, "Everyone else has one."

You may revisit the middle chapters when group chats, comparison, or sleep begin to shift.

You may lean on the later chapters when you are ready to say yes—or when you need to recalibrate after yes.

This is not about finding the "perfect" age.

It is about aligning **development with complexity**.

This book is about pacing.

About strengthening identity before amplification.

About building regulation before immersion.

About protecting connection while granting independence.

If you are looking for strict formulas, you will not find them here.

If you are looking for clarity, steadiness, and thoughtful leadership, this book is meant to support you.

Read it with curiosity.

Use what resonates.

Adapt what aligns.

Return when needed.

Because development is not rushed.

And neither is this conversation.

Core Philosophy

This was never about banning phones.
  It was about building capacity.

Strength before screens.

Identity first. Amplification later.

Friction is not harm.

Inconvenience builds resilience.
  Isolation requires action.

Capacity over comparison.

"Everyone else" is not a developmental standard.
  Regulation matters more than trends.

Delay is developmental.

Waiting builds muscles that instant access weakens.

Permission is a milestone.

A smartphone should signal readiness —
  not relieve anxiety.

Technology accelerates.

Childhood should stabilize.
　　You are not raising a child for today's group chat.
　　You are raising an adult for tomorrow's world.
　　Build strength.
　　Then expand access.

Reflection Questions for Parents

You do not need to answer all of these at once.

Some may feel relevant now.

Others may feel more meaningful a year from today.

Return to them when the conversation shifts in your home.

Readiness and Motivation

1. What does "readiness" truly mean in our family?

Is it defined by age, comparison, convenience — or **capacity**?

2. Am I delaying from fear or from clarity?

If fear is driving my decision, what specifically am I afraid of?

If clarity is driving it, what patterns am I observing?

Growth and Capacity

3. What signs of emotional growth have I noticed recently?

How does my child handle disappointment, exclusion, or frustration today compared to a year ago?

4. How does my child currently handle boredom?

Do they generate their own engagement — or rely on external stimulation?

5. What patterns concern me most right now — sleep, mood, distraction, comparison, conflict?

Which one deserves attention first?

Modeling and Influence

6. How does my own phone use model regulation?

What do my children observe about how I respond to notifications, conflict, and digital stress?

7. Where do I feel social pressure from other families — and how much influence should that pressure have?

Belonging and Identity

8. What kind of belonging do I want my child to build?

Is it based on constant access — or shared experience and identity?

9. In five years, what will matter more — the exact age of access, or the strength of my child's regulation and identity?

Integration and Structure

10. If my child received a smartphone tomorrow, would it expand their world — or shrink it?

What responsibilities would it support?

What vulnerabilities might it amplify?

11. Have I clearly explained my reasoning — or have I only enforced it?

Does my child understand the developmental purpose behind our timing?

12. If we were to say yes, what would gradual integration look like in our home?

What structure would protect both development and relationship?

Family Readiness Worksheet

Capacity Before Complexity

Use this worksheet as a quiet self-check.

There are no perfect scores — only patterns.

You may complete this alone or discuss it together as a family.

Part I — Emotional Readiness

Over the past 3–6 months, my child generally:

- ☐ Recovers from disappointment within a reasonable time
- ☐ Handles minor exclusion without prolonged spiraling
- ☐ Accepts boundaries without repeated escalation
- ☐ Can pause before reacting when upset
- ☐ Reflects on mistakes instead of deflecting blame

Notes:

Part II — Behavioral Readiness

My child currently:

- ☐ Completes responsibilities with increasing independence
- ☐ Manages shared screen limits without constant negotiation
- ☐ Protects sleep with reasonable consistency
- ☐ Follows through on agreed expectations
- ☐ Shows improvement in impulse control

Notes:

Part III — Social Readiness

In peer situations, my child:
- ☐ Can tolerate delayed responses without panic
- ☐ Navigates small conflicts without adult rescue
- ☐ Does not rely entirely on peer validation for mood stability
- ☐ Can be slightly different without collapsing socially
- ☐ Demonstrates growing confidence in identity

Notes:

Part IV — Family Alignment

In our home:
- ☐ We have clearly discussed expectations around devices
- ☐ We model reasonable digital habits ourselves
- ☐ We have a plan for sleep protection
- ☐ We are willing to recalibrate if needed
- ☐ Our decision feels grounded in clarity — not pressure

Notes:

Reflection

If access expanded tomorrow, would it:
- ☐ Expand responsibility and independence
- ☐ Primarily relieve social pressure
- ☐ Introduce stress we are not prepared for
- ☐ Strengthen coordination and trust

What feels most aligned right now?

Remember:

Readiness is not perfection.
It is consistency.
Capacity before complexity.
Identity before amplification.
Return to this worksheet as your child grows.
Timing is not fixed.
It is calibrated.

Teen Self-Readiness Reflection

Am I Ready for More Digital Freedom?

This is not a test.

There is no grade.

This is a self-check — for you.

Be honest. No one else needs to see your answers unless you choose to share them.

Part I — Emotional Regulation

When something happens online that I don't like, I usually:

- ☐ Pause before responding
- ☐ Think about whether it's worth replying
- ☐ Recover within a reasonable time
- ☐ Avoid posting when I'm angry
- ☐ Can let small things go

If I'm honest, when I feel ignored or left out, I tend to:

Part II — Impulse Control

I can:

- ☐ Put my phone down when I need to focus
- ☐ Stop scrolling without feeling irritated
- ☐ Sleep without checking notifications late at night
- ☐ Resist responding immediately to every message

☐ Complete responsibilities before using my phone

The hardest boundary for me right now is:

Part III — Identity & Validation

When I post something, I:

☐ Don't obsess over likes or views

☐ Don't let numbers determine my mood

☐ Don't compare myself constantly to others

☐ Feel secure even if a post doesn't get attention

☐ Know that social media shows highlights, not full lives

When I compare myself to others online, I usually feel:

Part IV — Conflict & Judgment

If someone posts something about me or argues with me online, I can:

☐ Stay calm

☐ Talk about it offline

☐ Walk away instead of escalating

☐ Admit when I'm wrong

☐ Repair if I've hurt someone

The last time I handled online conflict well, I:

The Bigger Question

If I had more digital freedom tomorrow, would I use it:

☐ To grow and connect responsibly

☐ To avoid boredom

☐ To seek validation

☐ To escape uncomfortable feelings

Be honest. There's no punishment here — only awareness.

Final Reflection

If I'm not fully ready yet, what skill do I need to strengthen?
If I am ready, what responsibility am I willing to accept in exchange?

Remember

Readiness isn't about age.
It's about regulation.
Freedom grows when responsibility grows.
The strongest digital users aren't the most connected.
They're the most self-controlled.

Family Digital Readiness Conversation

A Guided Discussion for Parents and Teens

This is not a debate.

It is not a negotiation.

It is a conversation.

Choose a calm time.

Sit at the table.

Phones away.

Each person answers honestly. No interruptions.

Step 1 — Parent Reflection (Parent Speaks First)

Parent:

Right now, what I notice about your growth is:

What makes me hesitate about expanding digital access is:

What makes me feel more confident about you recently is:

Step 2 — Teen Reflection

Teen:

What I feel ready for is:

What I struggle with sometimes is:

If I had more digital freedom, I would show responsibility by:

Step 3 — Shared Questions

Together discuss:

1. What does "readiness" mean in our family?
2. What would success look like 3 months from now?
3. What boundary feels most important right now?
4. What would trigger a reset or recalibration?
5. How can we protect sleep and real-world connection?

Write your shared agreements here:

Step 4 — The Exchange

More freedom requires more responsibility.

We agree that:

☐ Freedom increases when responsibility is consistent
☐ Sleep remains protected
☐ Conflict is discussed, not hidden
☐ Mistakes are repaired, not punished
☐ We can recalibrate without shame

Sign below not as a contract — but as commitment to growth.

Parent Signature: _______________________________________

Teen Signature: ____

Date: _______________________________

Remember

This conversation can happen more than once.

Readiness grows.

Boundaries adjust.

Trust builds gradually.

Digital maturity is not a moment. It is a pattern.

The Digital Milestone Ceremony

Marking the Transition With Intention

Most children receive their first smartphone like this:

A box.

A setup.

A password.

A download.

And then — life changes.

But growth deserves recognition.

If you choose to introduce a smartphone, consider marking the moment intentionally.

Not as surrender.

Not as relief.

Not as social compliance.

As transition.

Before the Device Is Activated

Sit together.

No distractions.

Parent, say something like:

> *"Today isn't just about getting a phone.*
>   *It's about the growth we've seen in you."*

Name specific strengths:
Your ability to handle disappointment.
Your improvement in responsibility.
Your growing independence.
Your steadiness in conflict.
Make the moment about character — not technology.

Acknowledge the Shift

Then say clearly:

> *"This device does not define you.*
> *It expands your responsibility."*

Explain that freedom and accountability grow together.
Not as threat.
As respect.

Teen Commitment

Invite your child to speak.
Ask:
What does this milestone mean to you?
What kind of digital user do you want to be?
How will you protect your sleep, your attention, your identity?
Let them articulate their own standards.
When young people say something aloud, it anchors internally.

The Family Agreement

Read aloud together:
We believe:

- Identity comes before amplification.
- Sleep is non-negotiable.
- Mistakes are repairable.
- Stepping away is strength.
- Character matters more than clicks.

You may even print and sign this page.

Not as a legal contract.

As a marker of maturity.

A Symbolic Gesture (Optional but Powerful)

You might:

Place the phone in their hands after a short conversation.

Offer a handshake — or a hug.

Take a photo of the moment (without posting it).

Write the date inside the cover of this book.

Small rituals create memory.

Memory creates meaning.

Meaning creates responsibility.

The Final Words

Before activation, say:

"You are ready not because of your age —
but because of your growth."

That sentence reframes the entire narrative.

The phone becomes earned trust.

Not overdue entitlement.

After the Ceremony

Set it up together.
Discuss first steps.
Agree on charging location.
Agree on usage windows.
Agree on check-ins.
Keep the tone calm.
This moment should feel steady.
Not anxious.
Not tense.
Grounded.

Why This Matters

Transitions without meaning feel casual.
Transitions with meaning feel significant.
And significance shapes behavior.
Years from now, your child may not remember the model of the phone.
But they may remember that it was handed to them with trust.
That it was framed as responsibility.
That it marked growth.
That is the point.

A Sample Family Digital Agreement

Built on Trust, Not Fear

This agreement is not about control.
It is about responsibility.
Digital freedom grows with maturity.
Maturity grows with consistency.
We agree to the following:

1. Sleep Is Protected

- Phones charge outside bedrooms at night.
- Devices are off at an agreed-upon time.
- Rest matters more than notifications.

Sleep protects mood, judgment, and self-control.
We treat it as non-negotiable.

2. Respect Is Expected

- We do not post or send what we would not say face-to-face.
- We do not screenshot or forward private messages without permission.
- We pause before responding when emotional.

Digital spaces require the same integrity as real life.

3. Mistakes Are Repairable

- If a mistake happens, we talk about it.
- We repair when needed.
- We recalibrate without shame.

Perfection is not expected.
  Responsibility is.

4. Boundaries Are Clear

- Devices are not used during family meals.
- Homework and responsibilities come first.
- Screen time is balanced with offline life.

Boundaries are not punishment.
  They protect attention and connection.

5. We Can Reevaluate

- Freedom increases with demonstrated responsibility.
- If patterns become unhealthy, we adjust calmly.
- Recalibration is part of growth — not failure.

Digital life evolves.
  So does maturity.

Our Shared Understanding

Technology is a tool.
  It is not a lifeline.
  It does not define identity.
  We believe:

- Character before clicks.
- Identity before amplification.
- Capacity before complexity.

Signed in commitment to growth — not perfection.

Parent Signature: _______________________________________

Teen Signature: _______________________________________

Date: _______________________________________

— FAMILY DIGITAL AGREEMENT —

Name: _________________________   Date: _______________

🎯 GOALS

- ____
- ____
- ____

☰ RESPONSIBILITIES

- ☐ ____
- ☐ ____
- ☐ ____

? REFLECTION QUESTIONS

- ☐ How can we create a healthy balance with **technology** in our family?
- ☐ What should you do if you feel **overwhelmed** or unsure online?
- ☐ What will you do if you or a friend encounter online bullying or unsafe?

MILESTONES

Responsibilities Earned:

- _____________________
- _____________________

Celebrations:

- _____________________
- _____________________

Signatures: _______________________________

Child Signature: ___________________________

Resources for Continued Learning

This book draws from lived experience, conversation, and research in child development and digital well-being.

For readers who wish to explore further, the following organizations and books offer additional perspectives.

Child & Adolescent Development

Center on the Developing Child — Harvard University
Research and educational materials on executive function, brain development, and emotional regulation.
developingchild.harvard.edu
American Academy of Pediatrics (AAP)
Guidance and policy statements on child health, media use, and development.
aap.org
Common Sense Media
Research summaries and media guidance for families navigating digital life.
commonsensemedia.org

Digital Well-Being

Digital Wellness Lab — Boston Children's Hospital
Research and resources on youth and digital media.
digitalwellnesslab.org
Center for Humane Technology

Exploration of how digital platforms influence attention and behavior.
humanetech.com

Wait Until 8th

A parent-led initiative encouraging thoughtful timing around smartphones.
waituntil8th.org

Recommended Reading

The Anxious Generation — Jonathan Haidt
On adolescence, social media, and mental health trends.
Digital Minimalism — Cal Newport
On intentional technology use and attention.
The Whole-Brain Child — Daniel J. Siegel & Tina Payne Bryson
On emotional regulation and developmental growth.
The organizations and books listed above are provided for informational purposes only and are not affiliated with or endorsing this publication.

Author's Note

I did not write this book as a technology critic.

I wrote it as a parent.

A parent who has sat at the dinner table watching a child glance toward a device that was not even in their hand.

A parent who has heard, "Everyone else has one," and felt the weight behind that sentence.

A parent who has wondered whether waiting builds strength — or unnecessary tension.

This book was not born from certainty.

It was born from questions.

What does readiness truly mean?

What is the difference between inconvenience and isolation?

How do we protect connection without surrendering intention?

What kind of adult are we preparing our children to become?

Those questions felt larger than a rule about smartphones.

They felt like questions about development, identity, and emotional regulation in an era that moves faster than childhood was designed to move.

I have watched children thrive with early access.

I have also watched children become quietly overwhelmed.

The difference rarely lies in the device itself.

It lies in timing.

In the steadiness of the adults guiding them.

In the strength of a child's internal foundation before immersion intensifies.

This book is not an argument for permanent delay.

It is not an argument against technology.

It is an invitation to slow the decision long enough to see clearly.

Because decisions made from clarity — rather than comparison — tend to age well.

If you are reading this, you likely care deeply.

You are not trying to resist the future.

You are trying to steward development responsibly.

That tension is real.

The culture of acceleration suggests that earlier is normal, faster is better, more connected is safer.

But development is not strengthened by pressure.

It is strengthened by pacing.

And pacing requires confidence.

There is no perfect timeline.

No universal age.

No formula that guarantees emotional stability in a digital world.

There are only patterns.

Capacity.

Observation.

Adjustment.

Conversation.

Repair.

Parenting in a digital age requires humility.

We are guiding children through environments we ourselves did not grow up navigating at this scale.

We are learning as we lead.

Discomfort does not mean incompetence.

It means awareness.

If this book offers anything, I hope it offers steadiness.

Not fear.

Not superiority.

Not rigid ideology.

Steadiness.

The steadiness to delay when delay aligns.

The steadiness to say yes when readiness emerges.

The steadiness to recalibrate when something feels off.

The steadiness to stand apart when necessary.

The steadiness to adjust without shame.

Above all, the steadiness to remember that your relationship with your child matters more than any device.

Technology will evolve.

Platforms will change.

Cultural norms will shift.

But your child's ability to regulate emotion, tolerate discomfort, and move through digital spaces with discernment — that is durable.

And that is worth building deliberately.

If, years from now, your child can step away from a screen without feeling diminished...

If they can navigate comparison without collapsing...

If they can recover from mistakes without unraveling...

If they can use technology without being used by it...

Then the timing debates will feel small in retrospect.

What will feel large is who they became.

Thank you for caring enough to ask hard questions.

Thank you for holding tension rather than reacting quickly.

Thank you for choosing thoughtfulness in a culture that rewards speed.

That choice is not loud.

But it is powerful.

About the Author

Jasvir Singh is an author focused on helping children and families build confidence, character, and emotional resilience in a rapidly changing world.

Drawing on conversations with students, parents, and educators, his books explore identity, integrity, self-regulation, and the quiet courage required to stand steady in a culture shaped by constant digital connection. Through both fiction and nonfiction, he emphasizes building internal strength before external validation.

He is the author of *Raising Confident Students*, *The Gift of Family Time*, and the middle-grade novels *The Only Vegetarian in Class* and *The Story of Two Kids: One Screen, One Dream.* His work encourages families to approach growth thoughtfully, prioritize connection, and navigate modern challenges with clarity and conviction.

Based in New York City, Jasvir continues to write books that support young people in developing grounded confidence and strong character—both online and off.

You can connect with me on:

🌐 https://jasvirsingh.com

Also by Jasvir Singh

Raising Confident Students

A Parent's Guide to Building Confidence, Communication Skills, Emotional Strength, and Everyday Courage

A practical and encouraging guide for parents raising thoughtful, resilient children.

Blending real-life insight with actionable strategies, this book helps families nurture confidence, communication, and independence—at home, in school, and beyond.

The Gift of Family Time

A Calm and Comforting Guide for Busy Moms and Dads

A gentle reflection for parents who love deeply but feel stretched thin.

This book reminds you that meaningful connection isn't built through perfection or grand gestures, but through presence, patience, and the quiet moments you already share. A reassuring companion for families navigating busy days with care and intention.

The Only Vegetarian in Class

A Middle Grade Novel About Kindness, Courage, and Finding Your Voice

Being different isn't easy—especially when you're the only one.

This heartfelt middle-grade story follows a young student navigating friendship, identity, and self-acceptance, showing how quiet courage and staying true to yourself can make all the difference.

The Story of Two Kids: One Screen, One Dream

A Story About Choices, Balance, and Life Beyond the Screen

Two kids face different paths in a world filled with screens.

As daily habits begin to shape their confidence, friendships, and dreams, they discover that small choices can quietly lead to very different futures. A meaningful and relatable story that encourages balance, discipline, and discovering life beyond digital distraction.

THREE GIRLS, THREE FUTURES

How Three Families Quietly Shaped Three Very Different Lives

A powerful story about how the quiet influence of family shapes our choices, relationships, and the lives we build.

www.ingramcontent.com/pod-product-compliance
Lightning Source LLC
Chambersburg PA
CBHW071508140726
47997CB00005B/1904